THE BEGINNER'S GUIDE TO THE OCCULT

THE BEGINNER'S GUIDE TO THE OCCULT

Understanding the History, Key Concepts, *and* Practices *of the* Supernatural

DEBORAH LIPP

ILLUSTRATIONS BY TRAVIS STEWART

ROCKRIDGE
PRESS

First Rockridge Press trade paperback edition 2021

Rockridge Press and the Rockridge Press logo are trademarks or registered trademarks of Callisto Media Inc. and/or its affiliates in the United States and other countries and may not be used without written permission.

For general information on our other products and services, please contact our Customer Care Department within the United States at (866) 744-2665, or outside the United States at (510) 253-0500.

Paperback ISBN: 978-1-64876-473-8 | eBook 978-1-64876-474-5

Manufactured in the United States of America

Interior and Cover Designer: Tricia Jang
Art Producer: Janice Ackerman
Editor: Samantha Holland
Production Editor: Rachel Taenzler
Production Manager: Holly Haydash

Illustrations © 2021 Travis Stewart. Author photo courtesy of Marshall Reyher.

10 9 8 7 6 5 4 3 2 1

TO
CLAUDINEY PRIETO,
MY DEAR FRIEND

Contents

INTRODUCTION
THE SECRET WORLD
OF THE OCCULT

I recently had to have an MRI for a shoulder injury. Although I'm not claustrophobic, the situation was extreme: the MRI machine was less than two inches from my nose, pressing tightly on both sides of my body. I tried some meditative techniques, but I was already so anxious and afraid that it was too late—I couldn't do it. I squeezed the panic button before I was all the way in.

The radiologist arranged for me to move to a different radiology center at the hospital—one with a larger machine. The center had rearranged its schedule for me, so I *had* to do it. As I waited, I breathed deeply, closed my eyes, and said, "Holy Guardian Angel, keep me calm through this procedure. Holy Guardian Angel, protect me from panic and fear." And, as I went in, I felt the protective calm of my Holy Guardian Angel with me. With a blindfold and earplugs, ignoring the hideous noise and uncomfortable space, I visualized the Kabbalistic Tree of Life and fell into a deep meditation.

Meditation, controlling one's thoughts, working with angels, and the Tree of Life, all of which helped me through this scary experience, are but a few areas of the vast world of occultism. Others include well-known areas such as astrology and tarot and more obscure ones like sigil-making.

"Occult," by definition, simply means secret, hidden, or mysterious. *The* occult refers to the world of such techniques and studies, from magic to alchemy, including the whole realm of the supernatural. This definition applies throughout this book, even though many astrologers, Wiccans, and rune workers may not consider themselves occultists. In the West, the occult became taboo during the rise of Christianity, when working with the supernatural was associated with the Devil, but the occult predates Christianity and has existed all over the world for millennia.

I have been an occultist for 40 years. I am, in no particular order, a witch, Wiccan, ritualist, tarot reader, bone reader, Pagan, magician, and Kabbalist. I've written books on Wicca, witchcraft, tarot, magic, and the elements (among other topics). At the time I first became Wiccan in 1981, the word "Wicca" was considered synonymous with witchcraft. Although there have always been witches who are not Wiccan, today, there are also Wiccans who don't consider themselves witches—but we'll get to that later.

All these beliefs and practices interconnect. The elements, for example, are prominently featured in Wiccan ritual, as well as in tarot, astrology, ceremonial magic, alchemy, and the Kabbalah. Ritual magic has a narrow definition (usually synonymous with ceremonial magic), but the performance of ritual permeates magic of all kinds.

So whether your interest is in spells, Paganism, astrology, or angels, you'll find value in surveying the occult as a whole. As you read, you'll find that any one of your occult interests is connected to others, and the overall study of the occult will give context and depth to each individual subject. Plus, you might find new subjects you love!

WHAT EXACTLY IS THE OCCULT?

In every part of the world and throughout history, there have always been mysteries, and there have always been people interested in those mysteries. Some of the questions we ask ourselves concern our being—for example, *Who are we? Why are we here? What is birth? What is death?* Others are questions about nature, natural phenomena, the sky, the stars, and the Earth. We might ask about fate and even about small things, like *What happens next?*

But many of the questions human beings ask come down to this: What does this life mean? Does it all tie together? Is there a wisdom behind it? From the dawn of time, these questions have cracked open the world. In asking them and seeking answers, and in studying, analyzing, and yearning to know more, human beings have developed both science and religion. We have also developed the occult.

The definition of the occult has changed over time, in part because the ideas and practices that are acceptable to the general public also change over time. For example, the use of foxglove as a healing herb was the provenance of the folk magician until digitalis was extracted from it to be used as medicine (it is still used today as a heart medication). Medicine, meteorology, astronomy, and chemistry were all born from the occult arts (or occult sciences). Once any one of them becomes generally acceptable in society, it is no longer "secret" or "hidden," and therefore no longer considered occult. (It's like how your favorite cool band achieves a megahit and then stops being cool.)

So what "counts" as occult today? You might think of it as synonymous with the supernatural, but the supernatural can refer to phenomena and events like hauntings, apparitions, and psychic occurrences. By contrast, when we use the term "the occult," we usually mean the *study* of those phenomena. An occultist is someone who works to gain mastery over the unseen.

As you scan the table of contents, you'll get a sense of what falls under the category of the occult: magic, witchcraft, astrology, alchemy, and divination—basically, any of the sciences developed to study or control the unknown world, when those facets of the unknown remain unacceptable to a rationalist or post-Enlightenment worldview. For instance, chemistry is no longer considered occult because, sometime after it split off from alchemy, it became mainstream.

In the West, the rise of the Roman Catholic Church in the Middle Ages drove the occult underground. Even the kindest of healing spells was suspected of coming from the Devil. Midwifery was long forbidden for the same reason (and because folk magicians were usually midwives), making childbirth more dangerous. Today, most people don't consider midwives to be satanic. You might be perfectly comfortable drinking an herbal tea for health. But sprinkle those same herbs in a circle around a laboring woman to help ease childbirth and suddenly it's seen as the occult. By contrast, in India, Ayurveda (traditional Hindu medicine) was never driven underground. And in China, astrology has been practiced for more than 2,200 years without being forced into hiding.

Fast-forward to the present day in the West: many occult arts have reemerged in a more respectable light. While people might mock astrology, they also pay attention to it. About half of Americans believe in psychic abilities and spiritual healing. Today, the commercialization of occult knowledge is flourishing. (Sephora, a global cosmetics retailer, even tried to market a "starter witch kit" in 2018.) Yet the occult largely remains hidden for the same reasons it started out as hidden: because few work to understand its depths. To choose to truly study it is admirable, and for those who make that choice, I hope this book is a helpful start.

RELIGION AND THE OCCULT

All religions have an exoteric and an esoteric side. The *exoteric* is public-facing and readily visible, while *esoteric* refers to the secret, hidden, obscure, and mystical side of the religion. For example, Christianity has Christian mysticism, Judaism has Kabbalah, and Islam has Sufism. A small percentage of the people who attend church, synagogue, or mosque have an interest in the esoteric side of their religion.

Mysticism, the seeking of an ecstatic or visionary state, isn't by itself the occult. No one thinks of Teresa of Ávila (a mystical and visionary saint of Renaissance Spain) as an occultist. But when mystics use specific studies, symbols, or rituals to achieve personal desires or spiritual goals, this can be considered occult. And it can be considered forbidden, even—perhaps especially—when it arises directly from religion.

Certain religions incorporate occult arts directly in their practice and can be seen as suspect as a result. Consider Wicca and the practice of witchcraft or magic; Wicca is a religion in which occult arts are normalized. Discomfort with the occult may be one reason some Wiccans separate themselves from witchcraft. What's more, in the West, we have a long and uncomfortable history of treating the religious practices of people of color as suspect and inferior. Being suspicious of their magic is part of that. Thus, in the West, Vodoun (Vodoun is the religion; voodoo is its magical practice) is perceived as evil, and African "witch doctors" are perceived as both dangerous and ridiculous.

Confusion and misunderstanding occur when we romanticize and co-opt the religious, mystical, or spiritual traditions of other cultures, which has happened to many Indigenous American spiritual customs. Even though the occult generally is looked down upon by many, the customs and practices typically associated with white Westerners are not demonized to the same extent. But whether it is treated with suspicion, as with Vodoun, or is simply unknown to people outside that religion, the occult has always been connected to religious practices.

SCIENCE AND THE OCCULT

Both the occult and religion emerged from the human need to ask questions. Science comes from this same curiosity. Occultists and scientists alike study, examine, contemplate, and experiment. Occultists and scientists alike form hypotheses, use controlled techniques, and draw conclusions, fine-tuning as they go.

In some cases, as a given science emerged, there was no "occult" part left. For instance, weather prediction is no longer considered occult, and there's no surviving occult art of meteorology. The science of meteorology became accepted and normalized. In other cases, a science emerged as an offshoot of the occult, for example:

- ◆ Chemistry emerged from alchemy. Robert Boyle (1627–1691), considered the first modern chemist, was an alchemist. So was Sir Isaac Newton (1643–1727).
- ◆ Astronomy and astrology emerged together as the study of the stars.
- ◆ Midwifery was once the work of folk magicians.
- ◆ Therapeutic touch is used by medical professionals but is in many ways the same as the occult practice of "laying on of hands."
- ◆ Many modern medicines emerged from the treatments provided by folk magicians: digitalis derived from foxglove was mentioned earlier; willow bark brought us aspirin; and opioids originate from poppy seeds.

The biggest difference between magic and science is that occult philosophy places great emphasis on the practitioner's state of mind. An alchemist seeking God can create gold, but an alchemist motivated by greed cannot. As you can see, intention matters.

By contrast, science assumes that intention is immaterial. To that end, when studying occult phenomena, scientists have attempted to remove state of mind as a factor. Consequently, you get Zener cards—the purposely neutral circle, squiggle, square, etc.

symbols used to test for ESP (extrasensory perception, or mind reading). Studies show that emotion and attention impact clairvoyance, but parapsychology attempts to be a "real" science by removing those factors.

Every science struggles with the observer effect—the need to eliminate the impact of an observer on an experiment. It turns out you really *can't* eliminate state of mind. Occultists don't try.

OCCULT PHILOSOPHY

When we talk about Western occultism (the primary focus of this book), we must start with occult philosophy. This book is in no way comprehensive; with so many topics to cover, delving too deeply into philosophy would be a distraction. But we at least have to know where we started and how we got here.

It all starts (as so many things do) with the Greeks, during the Hellenistic period. Hellenic religion was syncretic (acquiring and incorporating other religions), and Alexander the Great's conquests gave the Hellenic people plenty of religions (and other cultural materials) to acquire. The philosophy of Plato, in particular, absorbed all sorts of ideas, and Neoplatonism—a mystic offshoot of Platonic philosophy—emerged from it.

The blending of many different schools of thought created unique ideas, some of which were seen as heretical and forbidden. For example, Gnosticism (first to second century CE) was a heretical Christian sect, arising equally from Hellenic thought and Christianity. Gnostics sought knowledge (gnosis) of the supreme being, while believing the Earth was created by a lesser deity (the Demiurge).

Hermeticism, which emerged around the same time as Gnosticism, Neoplatonism, and other philosophical and religious systems, is perhaps the most important and influential stop in our quick journey through occult philosophy. It remained influential through the Renaissance and to today. The *Hermetica,* upon which

Hermeticism is based, are, supposedly, the writings of Hermes Trismegistus, a semi-mythological figure sometimes said to have been a contemporary of Moses from the Bible—although Hermes Trismegistus's writings were eventually dated to about 300 BCE (more than 1,300 years later).

The *Hermetica* is a huge collection covering alchemy, astrology, and magic (known as the "three parts of wisdom"), as well as philosophy. Hermeticism states that there is a single underlying truth and that true religion seeks this truth. Heaven is eternal and true, but the body, being impermanent, is not true. Hermeticism seeks to explore the heavenly truth. You've probably heard this key phrase of occult philosophy: "As above, so below." This is paraphrased from the part of the *Hermetica* known as the *Emerald Tablet*: "That which is above is like to that which is below, and that which is below is like to that which is above."

The first Kabbalists—great Jewish mystics, many of whom were alchemists—were influenced by both Hellenism and Hermeticism. In 1533, Heinrich Cornelius Agrippa published the *Three Books of Occult Philosophy*, the first great work of syncretism in Western occultism. This collection mixed Neoplatonism and Kabbalah for the first time. The books covered diverse topics such as the elements, numerology, ritual magic, angels, demons, names of God, astrology, and divination. (Incidentally, this was the start of occultists robbing Kabbalah of its Jewish roots, which I'll discuss more in chapter 6.)

Agrippa laid the groundwork for Western occultism by combining Greek, Jewish, and other streams of philosophy. These philosophical underpinnings are a part of the occult as it has been practiced ever since. Secret knowledge, the elevation of the self beyond the physical, and heresy (which simply means any religious opinion contrary to church dogma) all remain influential in occult philosophy.

WHY STUDY THE OCCULT?

Many people think the occult is obsolete. We have science and the Internet; and why bother with "laying on of hands" when modern medicine is so advanced? Why study astrology when *Voyager 1* and *Voyager 2* have visited the outer planets of our solar system? Despite these scientific advances, many reasons to study the occult remain.

First, we study the occult because life is full of mystery, and our minds remain curious. As we open doors of knowledge, human beings seem always ready to close others. Open religion, close heresy. Open science, close the supernatural. Some people are like housecats, always compelled to discover what's on the other side of every closed door, and that might be a good description for occultists.

Second, the history of the occult (see page 154) is a vast repository of incredible knowledge and exploration. Some of it went down a wrong or misguided path—such as the adamant homophobia and racism of certain occult writings. Throughout many centuries, and in many cultures, schools of thought have not always agreed with one another. But even with the contradictions, mistakes, and prejudices, there is enormous wisdom to be uncovered and there are many great minds who have preceded us in our quest to explore, understand, and empower.

Human expansion is another reason. Some explore the occult because conventional religion doesn't provide intimacy with God. Others study the occult because conventional knowledge doesn't deepen their understanding of the inner self. Still others seek power—not, I hope, in an ugly sense. Rather, humans can do and be more than we are told, whether that's through clairvoyance, magic, or telepathy, and the occult provides an entrée to that power.

Finally, and perhaps most importantly, many of the things you're already interested in have their roots in the occult. If you're interested in Wicca or you're fascinated by tarot cards or you read your horoscope daily, you are touching upon the occult. Each practice is the tip of a deep, deep iceberg. You may not stick with any one occult subject— and you may find numerology uninspiring or Kabbalah overly complex—but all are components of a whole, and knowing even a little about them will enrich the parts that are meaningful to you.

How to Use This Book

The Beginner's Guide to the Occult is just that: a guided introduction. I could fill a bookcase with compelling works on each subject covered here. The Further Reading & Exploration section on page 156 will help you deepen your study of topics that particularly fascinate you. In many ways, this book is like being given a guided tour of an amazing city. Once the tour is over, it's up to you to choose which neighborhoods to explore, which museums to visit, which restaurants to enjoy, and which parks to play in.

And the occult is truly an amazing city. The chapters in this book are presented in what I believe is a logical and historical order. We start with folk magic, the oldest form of magic, and move to witchcraft—in many ways folk magic's companion. From there, subjects are introduced as they historically build on one another: early numerologists knew astrology, early Kabbalists studied alchemy, and so on. Nonetheless, you *can* skip around if you feel the urge.

Western occultism is emphasized because it is there that the various subjects presented in this book are most deeply interconnected. We'll certainly cover other cultures, briefly visiting topics like Chinese astrology, Australian folk magic, and American hoodoo, but most of what we discuss originated in Europe or the Near Middle East. With so many subjects across time and space, this book cannot be a comprehensive study, but is rather a rich introduction to start your explorations.

The history of occultism is one that has typically been sexist, racist, antisemitic, homophobic, and classist. Some of the best and most important authors on certain subjects of the occult reflect some or all of these traits. We can reject the bigotry and still learn from great occultists of the past. Some readers never want to study, say, Aleister Crowley, because he was racist (among other things). But it would be impossible to review the subjects we're discussing without highly influential authors such as Crowley. While I'll present material with problematic elements, I'll be truthful about both the good and the bad in that material. I certainly won't present sexist, gender-essentialist, homophobic, racist, or antisemitic ideas as a necessary part of occultism.

With that said, let's start our guided tour!

CHAPTER 1

FOLK MAGIC

There is no culture or time in history where folk magic has not existed. Whether we are talking about hoodoo in the American South, the folk healers of the British Isles, or the Latin American *curanderos*, everyone, everywhere, has practiced folk magic—a native magical practice mixed with cultural customs. Sometimes it goes unnoticed because it is so very ordinary.

A few of the many names that folk magicians are known by include wise men/women, cunning folk, conjurers, *wicca/ wicce* (Britain), *curanderos* (Latin America), *sangomas* (South Africa), witch doctors (Africa), *jhākri* (Nepal), and *pellars* (Wales).

Throughout the world, cunning folk have always healed, performed love magic, and protected people from witchcraft. (We'll get into this more in chapter 2.) They were the good workers who protected against evil. In Africa and South Asia today, cunning folk still perform this function. By the Middle Ages, folk magic was frowned upon in the West because conjurers were thought to get their powers from the Devil. While they were tolerated for the most part, from time to time magical practice was made illegal, and some cunning folk were jailed.

There are several ways to look at folk magic:

- ♦ **WHERE:** The British Isles, Africa, Nepal, Italy, Scandinavia, and many more—all have cunning folk.
- ♦ **WHY:** Healing, finding lost objects, seeing the future, and midwifery are all common purposes, among many others.

- ♦ **HOW:** Folk magic has often been considered the realm of the illiterate or ignorant, but practitioners have used grimoires (texts on magic), religious texts, and astrology, along with other erudite practices, for hundreds of years.
- ♦ **WHO:** Professional cunning folk renowned for their practice were sought out by their communities, but everyday people also have always used commonplace magic on their own. Even today, we knock on wood or throw spilled salt over our shoulders. Ashkenazi Jews say *keinehora* to avert the evil eye. Many Italian men wear a *cornicello cornetto*— the little twisted horn that brings good luck and virility. These are magical acts. From carrying lucky charms to making a corn dolly for a plentiful harvest, folk magic has always been done by everyone.

Scholars often define folk magic as purely practical, without a spiritual component, but this isn't entirely accurate. In the West, folk magic can be based in Christianity (such as when Bible verses are incorporated). Folk magic can also be rooted in religious or spiritual systems—voodoo in Vodoun, rune magic in Norse folk religion, and so on—but the point is to get results: to heal, to protect, to harvest, and so on.

Folk magic has often been looked down upon by other magicians. It's called "low magic," in contrast to "high magic," the difference being that "high" (ceremonial or ritual) magic is done to commune with God or angels, while "low" magic is done to achieve specific, mundane goals such as healing, love, and fertility. But there's also a class divide. "Low" magic is seen as being done by the poor, the less educated, and those with fewer resources. "High" magic requires more equipment, expense, and free time.

Some scholars argue that modern terms such as "hedge witch" or "kitchen witch" don't describe folk magicians, because, they say, modernity has eliminated folk magic. I disagree. The essence of folk magic is rooted in the ordinary, combining systems and techniques as needed; it focuses on effectiveness and prioritizes results over ritual. Modern people can do this just as ancient people could. Let's explore what folk magic is and dive into some common practices.

NON–OCCULT OCCULTISM

Though one of the meanings of occult is "hidden," folk magic is often practiced in the open. Magic is certainly part of the occult, but in this case, it's not really a secret.

Unlike other forms of occultism, folk magic isn't particularly interested in the theory behind the work. Throughout history, it was common for a conjurer to blend psychology, even trickery, with "real" magic. If the placebo effect makes the spell work better, why not use it?

Folk magic also focuses on behavior. Other occult arts place a greater emphasis on the will of the magician, on concentration, and on intention. While these factors play a role, the emphasis here is on *doing* and *saying*. These behaviors draw on certain universal core principles: sympathetic, contagious, and imitative magic, and power from nature, objects, words, and spirits or gods. Let's discuss each of these.

SYMPATHETIC MAGIC

That which is like a thing *is* the thing. Sympathetic magic leverages this simple and powerful principle: it incorporates objects that "have sympathy" with the subject by resemblance, physical connection, or symbolism. To work magic from a distance, use sympathy: anything *like* me can *be* me and can be subject to your magic. So, a picture of me is like me. My astrological sign is like me. By extension, things that are like my sign are also like me: since I am a Taurus, Taurus is like me, and so are bulls.

Anything that was once a part of me has sympathy with me: for the purposes of magic, my hair and nail clippings are like me, and therefore *are* me.

MAGICAL CONTAGION

Magical contagion is sympathetic magic based on past contact. Anything you once touched retains some of your essence. So a folk magician can do magic using the dust from my footprint, because my foot was once there. Contagion works both ways: lots of old spells call for the magician to arrange for a person to step on or over a magical object, so that they "catch" the magic when they come in contact with it.

◇―― MEET ――◇
SIR JAMES G. FRAZER

Sir James George Frazer (1854–1941) was an anthropologist, folklorist, and author of the seminal work *The Golden Bough*. It was originally published in 1890, and the 1915 edition was twelve volumes, with a thirteenth added in 1936. (There is also a one-volume abridgement.)

The Golden Bough (which first coined the term "sympathetic magic") compiles folk customs, rituals, and myths. In the book, Frazer identified a dying-and-resurrecting Sun God cycle of the ritual year—one that scholars now say probably didn't exist, but which deeply influenced Wicca and Neo-Paganism (modern Paganism), as well as popular culture and art. Its collection of folklore, customs, magic, and rituals remains invaluable. Alas, the book is also full of racist and other bigoted attitudes.

IMITATIVE MAGIC

Imitative magic is magic that *imitates* a desired behavior. You can take two sympathetic or contagious objects and bind them together, and, by imitation, the spell causes binding of the two objects. Let's say someone glues a picture of me to a twenty-dollar bill. By imitation, money will stick to me. European folklore tells us that during Beltane, the Gaelic May Day festival, lovers would have sex in the newly planted fields to teach them (by imitation) how to be fertile.

NATURAL POWER

Natural power comes from things found in nature. Folk magicians are often herbalists, using plants in their work. Cunning folk discovered that willow bark eased pain long before science revealed that it contained acetylsalicylic acid (aspirin). Natural power can also be derived from colors, stones, elements, and locations, among other things.

Some folk magicians are also animists—they believe in, and rely on, the animating spirits of nature. The herbs, animals, winds, etc., are helpers—free agents who participate in the magic.

POWER OBJECTS

Some objects are considered to have inherent power, while other objects are imbued with power. To a Plains Indian, for example, a feather has its own power, whereas a pipe acquires power through its creation.

Folk magicians use a wide variety of objects in their practice, which vary greatly by time and place. You might think of a wand or a knife as traditional tools of magic, and you'd be right, but an astrological chart is also a power object, even though it doesn't go in the folk magic tool kit.

A FOLK MAGIC TOOL KIT

Folk magic often relies on found objects, or those that are easily sourced. You can use all sorts of items from around the house, but it's helpful to have some basic ingredients handy in your folk magic tool kit. Expect this starter kit to grow as you learn more!

CANDLES are one of the most common tools of magic. Start with all-purpose white ones and add colors as you find them. Tea lights are handy, but a candle you can carve or mark is more useful. Naturally, you'll need matches or a lighter, as well as candleholders.

A PEN AND PAPER set aside for magic will get plenty of use in written spells and charms.

A POWER-DIRECTING OBJECT—usually a wand or knife—can be a part of virtually any spell.

A PENDULUM OR DOWSER is a frequently used implement of folk magic. The pendulum is a weight (a stone or bead) at the end of a cord or chain. A dowsing rod is similar, but instead of a weighted bead, a stick—often forked—is used. A traditional dowser finds water, but lost objects or treasure can also be discovered using it.

Finally, **REFERENCE BOOKS**, such as those listed on page 156, will help you quickly look up the color, sign, element, herb, etc. that corresponds to the work you're doing. Some old reference books, such as the ephemeris needed by an astrologer, can now be replaced by apps and websites, but books are still your most reliable companions.

WORDS OF POWER

Words of power can include the names of God, gods, or angels, or they might be rhymes, either traditional ones or ones composed for the occasion. They might even be "barbarous words," referring to words of which the meaning is unknown. Cunning folk in Christian cultures have used Psalms in their magic for centuries, but Native

Americans, voodooists, and Neo-Pagans also use sacred words in their spells.

Many spell books contain words to use for magical purposes, sometimes (but not always) accompanied by detailed instructions. They were used for centuries by traditional conjurers, and they're used by modern magicians today.

GODS AND SPIRITS

Folk magicians frequently call on the power of spiritual beings. As with ceremonial magicians, we can see this as not necessarily religious in nature; they are *using* the inherent power of spiritual beings, not worshiping or venerating them. The practitioner may believe deeply in the spirit being called in a spell, but perhaps the spirit may be as much a tool to them as a knife or a cauldron.

The conjurer understands that these beings bring enormous power. Perhaps the entire spell is simply calling upon a god with an appropriate incantation. More likely, it is combined with other tools.

The approaches to magic delineated in this section—sympathy, contagion, imitation, nature, objects, words, and spiritual beings—are just some of those used by folk magicians. Others include music, dance, gesture, ritual, trance, and divination. Such approaches and tools are generally used in combination.

FOLK MAGIC CUSTOMS AROUND THE WORLD

There has never been a place on Earth where crops were planted or babies were born without the presence of wise ones helping them along. Every country and continent, and every period of history, has had folk magicians. This section offers a sampling of practices from different parts of the world and points of history. The diverse assortment is just a taste of the nearly infinite world of folk magic; the books listed on page 156 can provide more.

But before we go on, it's important to note that when we talk about the various cultures that practice folk magic, the subject of cultural appropriation inevitably arises. It should be obvious that a group with a history of being oppressed doesn't want to give away things of beauty, that are a part of who they are, to people belonging to the culture that historically oppressed them (and often still does). It's not hard to understand, nor is it difficult to honor.

A similar concept is that of a "closed practice." Some components of some cultures are explicitly spelled out as off-limits. Maori tattoos, for example, are meant for certain initiation ceremonies, not for just anyone who wants cool "tribal" ink. I was once on the verge of choosing a particular magical name before I learned it was reserved for initiates of a religion that was not my own. So I chose a different name. In the spirit of respect, this book will *not* be teaching you how to do Indigenous American medicine, Santería (an African diaspora religion that originated in Cuba), or traditional Jewish gematria (a form of numerology). There are many, many other practices to explore.

British Isles

Great Britain, Ireland, and adjacent islands comprise the British Isles. Ireland has a long history of folk magic and customs, many of which are still practiced today. Ireland is populated not just by people but by the *sidhe*, or the fairy folk. The land is alive with these beings, and they are treated with respect. To this day, the Irish avoid defiling fairy mounds and are careful not to invoke the *sidhe* out loud, as it is considered impolite or unsafe.

Cunning folk throughout the British Isles often helped clients with problems such as theft and witchcraft. For example, a magically empowered reflecting surface, such as a mirror, crystal, or bowl of water, was a widespread tool. The folk magician would have a client gaze into the reflecting surface until they saw the image of the person who had stolen from them or bewitched them.

A common anti-bewitchment technique involved fire. In some cases, a special powder would be burned in the home of the client to burn away the bewitchment. Often, the heart of an animal (a sympathetic substitute for the evildoer) would be stuck with pins and then burned to achieve the same effect.

◇◇

✧→— MEET ⊢—←✧
RONALD HUTTON

Professor Ronald E. Hutton (1953–) is a historian and folklorist at the University of Bristol. He is well-known in the modern occult and witchcraft communities for his extensive writings on Paganism, witchcraft, and folklore.

Hutton's books include *The Pagan Religions of the Ancient British Isles: Their Nature and Legacy*; *The Stations of the Sun: A History of the Ritual Year in Britain*; *The Triumph of the Moon: A History of Modern Pagan Witchcraft*; and *Shamans: Siberian Spirituality and the Western Imagination*. He has brought a scholarly eye to a subject often full of romanticism and conjecture.

◇◇

ANCIENT EGYPT

In Ancient Egypt, magicians made a variety of amulets, formed of stone or other materials, that combined with words of power to protect against evil. The Eye of Horus talisman (the Utchat) was commonly worn to bring strength, safety, luck, and health. It could be made of a variety of materials, such as wood, gold, or lapis lazuli (see the illustration on page xx). Note that a talisman is used to bring in positive energies, while an amulet protects from the negative.

Scarab beetles were important symbols to ancient Egyptians, as they were generally considered to be bringers of life and good fortune. In *Egyptian Magic*, author E. A. Wallis Budge writes: "...when a man wished to drive away...sorcery...he might do so by cutting off the head and wings of a large beetle, which he boiled and laid in oil. The head and wings were then warmed up and steeped in the oil of the āpnent serpent, and when they had been once more boiled the man was to drink the mixture."

Ancient Egyptians also believed the spirit of a being could be placed into a wax image, which then had magical power. There's a story about a wax crocodile over which words of power were recited, which turned the figure into a living crocodile that devoured the magician's enemy. Wax figures, imbued with words of power, could also be used to gain a lover.

Names were another important part of Egyptian magic; knowing someone's name gave you power over them because a name is a part of a person's soul, their *ka*. Thus, many spells involved writing down someone's name and performing magic on the written name.

North American Hoodoo

Hoodoo (also known as "conjure" or "rootwork") derives from the secret practices of enslaved Africans in America. It is an amalgamation of Central and West African traditions and West Indies magic, and it is influenced by the Bible, voodoo, Cherokee religion, and many other practices. Hoodoo originated during the slave trade in the seventeenth century and is still practiced today. Due to its origins, the practice of hoodoo by those not of African descent is considered cultural appropriation by many.

Like all folk practices, hoodoo relies on sympathetic magic: honey makes things sweet, pins hurt, fire burns things away, and parts of a person's body function as that person. Some practices unique to hoodoo include the use of floor washes, bottle trees, an emphasis on candle magic, and "throwing bones" as a divinatory technique.

The purposes of hoodoo spells often differ from those from Europe. All practitioners worldwide practice love and protection spells, but European conjurers also place a heavy emphasis on returning stolen property, protecting animals, and fighting witch-craft. Hoodoo has a different repertoire: sweetening someone's attitude, justice in court, drawing money, and driving away ene-mies. Hoodoo is inclusive of revenge and harming enemies, while most European practitioners called those spells witchcraft rather than folk magic. (In Europe and North America, the techniques—and sometimes the practitioners—are basically the same; the intent is what's different.)

◇→┤ MEET ├─←◇ MARIE LAVEAU

Marie Laveau (1801–1881) was a renowned Vodoun priest-ess, free woman of color, herbalist, voodoo and hoodoo magician, midwife, and celebrity. She sold herbs, charms, and gris-gris (magic herb bags), ministered to prisoners, told fortunes, and healed the sick. She also led both public and private Vodoun ceremonies.

In addition to her Vodoun faith, she was a devout Catholic. The integration of Catholic prayer and holy water into her magic made it more acceptable to her upper-class white customers. Laveau's fame, beauty, and magical skill make her an object of fascination to this day, and her grave remains a popular tourist site in New Orleans.

FOLK MAGIC IN ACTION

Cunning folk protect from evil, accidents, and ill health; bring love; heal the sick; protect women and infants during childbirth; find lost or stolen objects; protect crops and animals; uncover thieves; read the future; interpret dreams; and protect professions (hunters, farmers, and sailors). Let's look at some specific examples.

HEALING

Healing is probably the most frequent subject of folk magic. The following is just a small sampling of examples of healing with folk magic. The books mentioned along with these anecdotes are rich sources of many more.

- **FOURTH-CENTURY ROME:** *The Golden Bough* records a cure for tumors used by Marcellus of Bordeaux, court physician to Theodosius I: "Take a root of vervain, cut it across, and hang one end of it round the patient's neck, and the other in the smoke of the fire. As the vervain dries up in the smoke, so the tumour will also dry up and disappear."
- **TWELFTH-CENTURY FRANCE:** Many French folk cures were related to the relics of saints. *Medieval Folklore* states that in Corbeny, Saint Marcoul was associated with healing. Monks immersed the relics of Saint Marcoul in water and sold the water in small bottles. Purchasers would wash sores with the water or drink it for a cure.
- **NINETEENTH-CENTURY GERMANY:** As mentioned in *The Golden Bough,* to prevent future dental problems and toothaches after having a tooth removed, it was recommended to insert the tooth into a mouse's hole.
- **NINETEENTH-CENTURY GREECE:** To cure jaundice, according to *The Golden Bough,* people were instructed to put a piece of gold in some wine, then expose the wine

to the stars for three nights and drink three glasses of the wine daily until the jaundice was gone.

♦ **EARLY TWENTIETH-CENTURY BRITISH ISLANDS:** In *Cecil Williamson's Book of Witchcraft,* it was recommended to carry the tip of a donkey's ear in a little cloth bag around the neck to protect against coughs, sore throats, and a hoarse voice.

Please note that the recommendations in this book are not intended to cure any disease or replace your current medications. Always consult with your doctor before embarking on a new healing protocol.

TRY IT YOURSELF

A HEALING SPELL

Magic workers will always be asked to heal. This simple spell combines several folk magic techniques: a power object, natural power, a sympathetic connection, words of power, and the invocation of a spiritual being. Depending on your preference, use God, a specific Pagan deity whom you worship, or another spirit, or rewrite step four entirely.

YOU'LL NEED:

- A candle (blue for healing or all-purpose white) and candleholder
- A knife or pin
- About a tablespoon of olive oil
- A picture of the person being healed
- A sprig of fresh rosemary
- An altar (a dedicated surface on which to place the candle and photo)

INSTRUCTIONS:

1. Prepare the candle by carving the name of the person to be healed into it with the knife or pin. Then "dress" the candle by rubbing it with the olive oil. Using counterclockwise and downward movements, say, "Sickness, sickness, away, away."
2. Prepare the photo by rubbing fresh rosemary on it. Using upward movements, say, "Healing, healing, stay, stay."
3. Place the candle and picture on the altar, upon which you may have other items and/or incense. Light the candle.
4. Repeat the following nine times: "God burn illness to ash, God bring healing fast."
5. Let the candle burn completely down.

Protection and Good Fortune

It's not necessary to reach into antiquity for good-luck folk magic; these practices survive today. A kiss at the stroke of midnight on New Year's Eve brings good luck now, just as it did in ancient Rome. Here are some present-day good luck and protection traditions from around the world:

- **MEXICO:** Wreaths (*ristras*) are hung in homes for protection, luck, and wealth and are typically made of of chiles or garlic. Some are only the spice, drying for later use in cooking while also bringing protection. Others are just for magic and include things like pictures of saints, packets of magical herbs, lodestones, rock salt, pine nuts, and fresh aloe.
- **CHINA:** Folklore says bamboo drives away evil spirits and calls forward good spirits. Making a flute out of bamboo, carving the name of a good spirit into the flute, and then playing it calls the spirit to you.
- **SRI LANKA:** The plant called *be-still* is known as "lucky beans" and is worn as a talisman.
- **IRELAND:** The Irish know that every home has a spirit, and keeping that spirit happy keeps the home happy. Have you ever lost your keys only to find they're exactly where you looked first? The house spirits are playing pranks, indicating they're none too pleased with you. To appease house spirits, keep your home clean, be welcoming to visitors, and leave offerings. Always have enough food and drink for unexpected guests—hospitality is an important virtue to house spirits.

Lost Objects

In *Cunningham's Encyclopedia of Magical Herbs*, Scott Cunningham says, "To find a lost object, mix poke with hydrangea, violet, and galangal. Sprinkle this around the area where the article was last seen." Cunningham also suggests burning stillingia and following the smoke to a lost object's location. (Also known as queen's root, stillingia is native to the southern United States prairies and was used in Indigenous American folk medicine.)

Dowsing rods can also be used to find lost objects, as well as water and treasure. The ancient Chinese, Greeks, and Romans dowsed, and it is mentioned in the Book of Exodus. A cave painting in Tassili n'Ajjer, a national park in Southeastern Algeria, shows what looks like a prehistoric dowsing rod.

To dowse, a Y-shaped stick or rod is often used; you hold an arm of the V section in each hand and allow the base to point you in the proper direction. Presumably, the rod has been blessed or empowered in some way, and the dowser is perhaps using a prayer, invocation, charm, or some other form of personal preparation.

A pendulum, which typically works with "yes or no" responses, is another folk magic implement for finding lost or stolen property, but it has many uses. Before the days of sonograms, pendulums were used to determine the sex of fetuses, with "boy or girl" replacing "yes or no."

Before beginning work with a pendulum, most people today ask, "Show me yes" and "Show me no." Traditions about the meaning of vertical, horizontal, or circular movement vary widely. As with dowsing, the implement is typically blessed or charmed, and you might begin with a prayer or spell.

There are two techniques to find property using a pendulum: One is to walk with the pendulum, following in the direction of "yes" movements. The other is to hold the pendulum over a map and allow it to guide you. If you lost something in your home, you might use a floor plan or sketch instead of a map.

FOLK MAGIC EVERYWHERE

Folk magic is the oldest form of magic. Cunning folk have always existed, and it has always been true that human beings have had a repertoire of customs that we'd now call "magic" or "superstition." The enormous range of folk magic practices includes healing, bringing luck, and protection from evil.

Folk magic is sometimes not considered part of the occult, but we've learned that folk magic is indeed mystical and mysterious, despite its roots in the ordinary, and often overlaps with other occult arts. For example:

- Wise people may call upon spiritual beings, just as ceremonial magicians, alchemists, and other occultists do. The names of God, angels, and demons figure prominently in ceremonial magic.
- Cunning folk use astrology, grimoires, and other books of magic.
- Both folk magicians and alchemists use the power of plants and minerals.

As you proceed through this book, ask yourself if each practice you learn about is different from, or connected to, folk magic: Would a conjurer have used this technique in the past? Do folk magicians use it today?

WITCHCRAFT

Beginning as the dark flip side to folk magic, witchcraft has changed and transformed throughout history, like the shape-shifter it is. Today, it has become almost impossible to know what someone means when they say the word "witch." As we've learned, one of the jobs of the folk magician was to combat bewitchment. So how did we go from there to bumper stickers that say things like "Witches Heal"? Let's explore.

Around 906 CE, the Church document *Canon Episcopi* indicated that "certain wicked women perverted by the Devil" worshipped the Pagan goddess Diana in the night. This began the process of lumping any surviving Pagan worship or practice in with Satan worship and witchcraft. Then, in 1484, Pope Innocent VIII issued an edict that launched witch hunts in full force. Healing practices, which were basically unpunished by the Church, were now lumped in with the magic that witches were accused of using. While village healers were mostly left alone, if you *were* accused of witchcraft, you would be forced to confess to healing, as well as cursing cattle and having sex with the Devil.

A few hundred years later, Increase Mather—a Puritan clergyman influential in the Salem witch trials—explicitly said that healing came from Satan and not God. Take Isobel Gowdie (see page 20). Her remarkable confessions under torture are among the most famous in the long period of witch hunts. In addition to saying she had sex with the Devil, shape-shifted, and cast spells that spoiled crops and killed children, she "confessed" to healing sickness more than 25 times.

This muddies the water: Is a healer a folk magician or a witch? The Church had it both ways for so long that it became easy to define a "witch" as a practitioner not of evil but of the forbidden. Witches were redefined as outcasts, and sure enough, that eventually made them "cool." Be aware, though, that redefining witchcraft happened in Christian Europe. In much of the rest of the world, especially Africa and South Asia, "witch" still means "evildoer," and witch hunts continue. In Ghana, the Akua Denteh Foundation was formed in 2020 to combat attacks against women accused of witchcraft (named for Akua Denteh, who was lynched for witchcraft in July 2020).

Ronald Hutton's book *The Triumph of the Moon* documents how the combination of certain cultural forces in England—a reawakening awareness of nature and nature worship, the occultism of the late nineteenth and early twentieth centuries, and a desire for wildness and the forbidden among the people—combined. The English landed on the label "witch" as the most fitting descriptor of those so awakened.

In the end, we're left with a lot of different people who mean a lot of different things, all using the word "witchcraft" to mean them. As you read on, you'll find out more about those people, who they were in the past, and who they are today.

◇→┤ MEET ├←◇
ISOBEL GOWDIE

Little is known about Isobel Gowdie herself. The extraordinary details of her four confessions of witchcraft in 1662 provided unusually rich insight into folk magic and the folklore of witchcraft. Nearly two hundred years later, these confessions were published in Robert Pitcairn's *Ancient Criminal Trials in Scotland*. Gowdie's confessions were discussed at length in Margaret Murray's *The Witch-Cult in Western Europe* and have been the subject of novels, plays, and music.

UNDERSTANDING WITCHCRAFT TODAY

So how do we know what is meant by "witchcraft"? Let's begin by looking at who, today, would consider themselves witches. What practices and ideas do witches have in common? Mixing together so many variations may seem like I'm overgeneralizing—there are doubtless innumerable exceptions—but it creates a basic understanding.

MAGIC AND SPELLS

Practicing magic is *the* defining feature of witchcraft. If you don't cast a spell, make a charm, or do some form of magic, you're not a witch. But *how* you do magic varies widely.

The modern coinages "hedge witch" or "kitchen witch" refer to a practice basically indistinguishable from folk magic. Such witches focus on herbalism and on the homemade. While a Wiccan might have a consecrated knife (an "athame"; see page 31) used only for magic, a kitchen witch might pull any knife from the drawer for her spell. A "green witch" is similar, but may focus more on wildcrafting and may have an animistic relationship with plants and nature— that is, may commune with them as sentient beings.

While any witch might use herbs in spells, they might also use stones and crystals, written or spoken words, elaborate or simple rituals, drumming, dance, or many other practices. Most witches see themselves as practitioners for the good, but many are willing to curse, coerce, or control with their magic. Witchcraft as an art is morally neutral and depends on the specific practitioner.

ENERGY WORK AND TRANCES

Most witchcraft involves an altered state of consciousness (such as trance) at least some of the time. Some witches think of themselves as shamans, although that term has a specific anthropological meaning that does not include self-taught Europeans or non–Indigenous Americans.

There is a strong historical association with magical trance and drug use, especially inhalation of psychotropic incenses. Some witches today include drug use among the techniques used to induce trance. Trance practices may include astral travel and other forms of noncorporeal journeying, possession, mediumship or "aspecting" (channeling), and dream work.

Energy work performed by witches can refer to any number of practices, from laying on of hands to working with the aura (the human energy field) to sending energy as a form of magic. Shooting bolts of energy from your hands doesn't look as cool in real life as it does when Doctor Strange does it, but it's a time-honored method of spellwork. Healing can be performed by sending energy in a certain direction or by interacting with the patient's energy.

COVENS AND SOLITARY PRACTICES

Witches may work either solitarily or in covens (groups of witches who gather regularly). In the highly influential book *The Witch-Cult in Western Europe*, Margaret Murray defined witches as always working in a coven of thirteen: six men, six women, and an officer of either gender. Modern covens may be of any number of members, although most consider thirteen a maximum. Some covens care about the gender of their members, and others do not.

OTHER OCCULT PRACTICES

Most witches do not limit themselves to practices strictly defined as witchcraft and are conversant in at least a few other aspects of the occult. Witches may be tarot readers, astrologers, Kabbalists, or even alchemists. Any of these occult practices may then be incorporated into their witchcraft. Additionally, witches may be members of one or more other occult organizations, such as the Freemasons, Thelemites, and Rosicrucians.

Additional practices that are magical, spiritual, or energetically focused may reach beyond Western occultism, and might not even be considered occult at all. A few such practices of witches I know include hoodoo, reiki, yoga, ayahuasca ceremonies, and tantra.

WITCHCRAFT AND RELIGION

A witch may or may not be religious. A religious witch may or may not mix religion and witchcraft. Some witches go to church on Sunday and then come home and practice what is essentially a secular witchcraft. For others, witchcraft is mixed with religion, and this can take multiple forms.

In the religion of Wicca, witchcraft is an inherent part of worship. There are Wiccans who say they are not witches and do not practice witchcraft, but even in a religion that is less than 100 years old, this is an incredibly new phenomenon, and I'd argue that it's at odds with the very definition of Wicca (which comes from an Old English word for "witch").

Religion may also be practiced side by side with witchcraft. Some consider "Christian witch" an oxymoron, while others identify as such comfortably. Jesus or the saints may be incorporated on a Wiccan altar or in a spell. Deities of other Pagan religions may be incorporated into witchcraft as well.

Finally, one may engage in many types of practice at once. A Wiccan may also be a Heathen (a follower of Norse Paganism), keeping the two separate or not. I may go to synagogue on Friday night and practice with my Wiccan coven on Saturday night. Witchcraft is remarkably flexible in its spirituality.

WHICH WITCH?

The historical changes wrought upon the word "witch" leave us needing to define each one. Today, you might encounter people using this word to mean any the following. Screenplay writers are remarkable at creating characters who fall into all these descriptions at once.

PRACTITIONERS OF EVIL

This is the original understanding of "witch." In the Middle Ages in Europe, the assumption was that this was because witches had made a pact with the Devil—a belief that persists to this day. Two examples of witches who might be considered "practitioners of evil" are Agnes Sampson and Isobel Gowdie (see page 20).

Burned for witchcraft in Scotland in 1591, Agnes Sampson confessed, after being asked by a woman to get rid of her father-in-law, as noted in the United Kingdom's National Archives document "A Witch's Confession," that "she made a picture of wax and raised a spirit at a waterside beside a brier bush, desiring her to enchant it to serve for his destruction, and send it to the said woman to be put under his bed sheet or bed head."

One of Isobel Gowdie's confessions was that "She attempted to destroy her neighbour, Bradley's crops by taking a child's body from the grave and using it as part of an incantation." And "she used effigies of the Laird of Park's male offspring to cause them death or suffering."

OUTCASTS, REBELS, AND PRACTITIONERS OF THE FORBIDDEN

Once healing and witchcraft became conflated, witchcraft could be considered anything that made people uncomfortable. Witchcraft was feared by those in authority and could be seen as the natural weapon of the oppressed. After all, it was available to anyone with the skill to practice it and needed no official sanction.

In 1899, folklorist Charles Godfrey Leland published *Aradia, or the Gospel of the Witches*. This was a book of spells and lore of Italian witches, provided to Leland by a woman he called Maddalena. It tells that Aradia, daughter of the goddess Diana and her brother Lucifer, was brought into the world to be the first witch. The purpose of witchcraft, Diana says, is to fight the oppressors. Witchcraft is transformed from evil to activism—witches aren't mere poisoners; they are poisoners of authorities, including Church authorities, who perpetrate oppression.

✦⤞ MEET ⤝✦
MATTHEW HOPKINS

Matthew Hopkins (circa 1620–1647) was a notorious witch-hunter, self-styled "Witchfinder General," and the author of the witch-hunting document *The Discovery of Witches*. His accusations and tortures resulted in the confessions and subsequent executions of at least 230 alleged witches in England, more than in the previous 100 years.

Hopkins's methods of torture included sleep deprivation, "pricking" (sticking knives or pins in supposed "Devil's marks"—moles or skin discolorations), and "swimming" (tying the accused to a chair and throwing them in the water—a witch would be "rejected" by water and float). His book became a manual that guided the New England witch hunts.

From Fiction to Feminist Icon

In fiction for most of modern history, only villainous women had power. Femmes fatales sorceresses, and poisonous hags were interesting, whereas "good" women were silent and demure. Snow White barely speaks in her own movie; it's the Evil Queen who gets the castle and the Magic Mirror.

In the twentieth century, feminists noticed this and embraced it. In 1968, Women's International Terrorist Conspiracy from Hell (W.I.T.C.H.) was formed. As quoted by Margot Adler in *Drawing Down the Moon*: "WITCH is . . . theater, revolution, magic, terror, joy, garlic flowers, spells. It's an awareness that witches and gypsies were the original guerrillas and resistance fighters against oppression—the oppression of women."

It's unclear if the women of W.I.T.C.H. were aware that Wicca had already been in the United States for a few years. Nevertheless, the witch as an icon, symbol, and metaphor was embraced by a feminism and a women's spirituality movement that didn't always take the idea of witchcraft literally.

Wicca and "Traditional" Witchcraft

Modern Pagan witchcraft, or Wicca, emerged in 1954 with the publication of *Witchcraft Today* by Gerald Gardner. It was (and is) a unique combination of folk magic, occultism, and Pagan worship: both a "Craft" and a religion. (Wicca picked up the habit of calling its art "the Craft" from Freemasonry.) Many have said that Gardner made it all up, but research by writer Philip Heselton establishes the existence of the New Forest Coven, although their roots don't go back further than about the 1920s.

The coven consisted of occultists with interests similar to Gardner's—they were Rosicrucians, herbalists, folklorists, psychics, and nature worshippers who were interested in Margaret Murray's "witch cult." Gardner took their rich blend of occult ingredients, added his own knowledge of Indigenous ceremonies from

◇→ MEET ←◇
GERALD GARDNER

Gerald Brousseau Gardner (1884–1964) was an occultist, folklorist, and witch who popularized, publicized, and promoted a new form of witchcraft—Wicca. Living in Malaya, in Southeast Asia, from 1911 to 1936, he witnessed Indigenous magical rituals. When he returned to England, he met and was initiated into the New Forest Coven.

Gardner's occult interests included Theosophy, Rosicrucianism, Freemasonry, psychic phenomena, druidry, and Thelema. His most influential books were the novel *High Magic's Aid* and the nonfiction books *Witchcraft Today* and *The Meaning of Witchcraft*. To the chagrin of his coven, Gardner never met publicity he didn't like, and his promotions almost single-handedly created the modern witchcraft movement.

Southeast Asia and a familiarity with magical lodges (see page 120), and created what he called "reconstructed" rituals. He formed the Bricket Wood Coven, with such influential members as authors Doreen Valiente, Jack Bracelin, and Fred Lamond, and a movement was born.

Several witchcraft traditions eschew the term "Wicca" and are more steeped in folk magic and nature, with less occult-style formality of ritual. Some of these emerged around the same time as the Gardnerian tradition. These traditions include Cochrane's Craft, 1734 Tradition, Feri Tradition, and Y Plant Bran. They remain a minority among witches, most of whom recognize Wiccan structures as a model. Let's take a closer look at British Traditional Wicca and Eclectic Wicca, which are alive and well today.

BRITISH TRADITIONAL WICCA

Gardner helped form multiple covens. "Gardnerian" was coined as an insult to Gardner and his coven, but it stuck, and many thousands of Gardnerian witches practice the tradition today. (In Wicca, "tradition" is roughly equivalent to "denomination.") The Wicca practiced by Gardnerians, Alexandrians, and a few others is often called British Traditional Wicca and has specific characteristics that defined Wicca in general until about the 1990s:

♦ **INITIATORY:** A person is not a member of the tradition until they have gone through the ceremony of initiation.

♦ **LINEAGE-BASED:** The only people authorized to perform initiations are those who were themselves properly initiated, in a lineage tracing back to one of Gardner's priestesses (for a Gardnerian), Alex Sanders (for an Alexandrian), or whomever is the source of the tradition.

♦ **HIERARCHICAL:** Covens are led by a high priestess in partnership with a high priest, and the leaders have authority over how the coven is led and who will be initiated.

♦ **SECRET:** Initiates swear an oath of secrecy, keeping private the exact rituals, god names, and members of the coven, among other things.

By the 1970s, a number of traditions that functioned along these lines had been manufactured. Often, these traditions had fabricated origin stories—now fondly (if sarcastically) called "grandmother stories"—tracing them back to ancient times. With a little bit of fakery, sincere and magical traditions were born, many of which still exist.

ECLECTIC WICCA

By the 1970s in the United States, the demand for Wicca was vastly outstripping the supply that a lineage-based tradition could handle. Americans are a freewheeling bunch, and Wicca began to take on a decidedly do-it-yourself bent. A breakthrough came in 1989 in the form of Scott Cunningham's book *Wicca: A Guide for the Solitary Practitioner*, probably the best-selling book on the subject.

Wicca advocated a Craft based on intuition and a freedom to make it up as you go along; it allowed for self-initiation (an oxymoron in traditional Craft) and focused on practicing alone. This meant that anyone who *wanted* to be Wiccan *could* be Wiccan. Eclectic Wicca—usually solitary, sometimes coven-based—is creative, expressive, and accessible, although it lacks the hereditary knowledge base of older traditions.

PRACTICING WITCHCRAFT

The variations of witchcraft are, as we've seen, enormous. For example, if you were a feminist witch in 1968, you'd be performing political theater. If you were an Italian witch in 1899, you might be poisoning your oppressors. Certain practices, though, are universal, which we'll learn about next. In addition to discussing a wide range of practices, I'll zero in on Wicca, arguably the most widespread form of witchcraft.

Casting a Spell

Witchcraft is fundamentally the practice of magic and spellcasting. I've written three books on casting spells. It's tricky to narrow it down to the basics, but fundamentally, magic involves a combination of the focused mind and will of the witch and a set of tools and ingredients (including those described on page 31) that help generate power, which is then sent to the target of the spell. In the healing spell on page 14, for example, the tools and ingredients include the candle, the picture, the herbs, and the words spoken. The target is the person being healed. You focus, concentrate, raise energy, and send it. That's a spell in a nutshell.

Casting a Circle

Circle casting is a core part of Wicca—it is how all rituals start. (Not all witches are Wiccan, of course, and spells don't *require* cast circles.) The circle protects, and it contains energy like a pressure cooker, so that it can build powerfully before it is released.

Wicca and other new witchcraft traditions in the early twentieth century were started by occultists with a strong ritual background. They were inheritors of the full range of practices described in the timeline on page 154. Circle casting draws on elements of Enochian magic, magical lodges, and the Golden Dawn (see chapter 7).

There's enormous variety in how this is done—which tools are used and in which order, which direction you start in, and so on. The basics go like this:

1. Each of the four cardinal points of East, South, West, and North (the "quarters") are marked, generally with a candle.
2. A circle is drawn upon the ground, in the air, or both, with the quarters at the perimeter. A tool such as the athame, wand, sword, or staff is used for this.

A WITCH'S TOOLS

Numerous tools are associated with witchcraft. Some have changed over time, and some are evergreen. Let's look at some common tools witches use.

Your first image of a witch probably includes a **BROOM** and a **CAULDRON**. Historically, brooms were phallic symbols—and not always just symbols! Today, brooms are used magically to sweep away negativity, and they are ceremoniously jumped at handfastings (Wiccan weddings). As for **CAULDRONS**, they can be used to contain a fire as well as a magical brew. They can be pricey, though, and many witches don't have one.

There are four tools that are shared by Wicca, ceremonial magic, and the tarot: the **SWORD**, **WAND**, **CUP**, and **PENTACLE** (a disk or plate with a five-pointed star on it). These are associated with the four elements of Air, Fire, Water, and Earth, and they aid in magic related to each element. They help form ritual space and direct energy.

A witch's knife is known as an **ATHAME**; it is usually black-handled and double-edged.

Most witches have a **DIVINATION TOOL** of some kind—a tarot deck, crystal ball, black mirror, etc.; there are dozens of options.

For some Wiccans, the **BOOK OF SHADOWS** is passed down as part of one's initiatory heritage and may be secret. Often handwritten, this text is unique to each tradition and sometimes to each individual witch. For others, it's merely the notebook used to record spells and rituals.

Many other tools are used only by one tradition or only occasionally. For example, the **STANG** (a forked wand of specific construction) is generally only used in Cochrane's Craft as a kind of portable altar.

3. The circle is sprinkled and censed, meaning cleansed with salt water and incense.

4. Beings of the quarters, each generally associated with one of the four elements, are summoned for protection. (Some people summon the fifth element of Spirit at the center.)
5. While each step is done, words of power and intention are spoken.

Once the circle is cast, magic, worship, and other witchcraft can be performed. When the rite is finished, the steps are carefully reversed, and the circle is declared open.

LUNAR RITES

Witchcraft, religious and otherwise, is deeply tied to the moon. Witches time spells by moon phases to take advantage of lunar energies. The waxing moon is for spells of increase (bringing wealth, health, and opportunity), and the waning moon is for spells of decrease (causing things to go away).

Most Wiccans worship at the full moon; some also do so at the new moon. After the circle is cast, praise and offerings to the goddess of the moon are given. Ideally, this would take place outdoors in the moonlight. When indoors, you would face the direction of the rising moon. Ask the moon to be present, dance and sing in her praise, and consecrate cakes and wine in her honor, pouring out the first for her (set aside to pour out later if you're indoors). Non-Wiccan witches might skip the cast circle and just dance by moonlight.

MAGICAL CLEANSING

It's important to cleanse your tools of past energies and consecrate each tool to its purpose. Here's how:

YOU'LL NEED:

Stick incense and a holder, or loose incense and a charcoal on a brazier

Matches or a lighter

Small dish of water

Small dish of salt

A tool to be cleansed

Your athame or wand (if you have one)

An already-consecrated tool (if you have one)

INSTRUCTIONS:

1. Point your athame, wand, or hand at the incense and say, "Air, bring wisdom."
2. Light the incense using matches or a lighter and say, "Fire, bring power."
3. Place your athame, wand, or hand in the water and say, "Water, bring cleansing."
4. Place your athame, wand, or hand in the salt and say, "Earth, bring grounding."
5. Mix three pinches of salt into the water.
6. Pass the tool through the incense smoke, end to end, and say, "Air and Fire, cleanse and consecrate this [tool]."
7. Wet the tool with salt water, and say, "Water and Earth, cleanse and consecrate this [tool]." (If the tool can be damaged by salt water, clean it thoroughly after you're done.)
8. If possible, touch the tool to an already-consecrated one to use magical contagion.
9. Say, "So be it," and immediately use the tool to seal the consecration.

THE WHEEL OF THE YEAR

Wiccans celebrate eight solar holidays, known collectively as "the wheel of the year." Lunar ceremonies are known as "Esbats," and holidays are "Sabbats." Sabbats tend to focus on the god of Wicca, whereas Esbats focus on the goddess. The following table shows the dates and what they symbolize.

SABBAT	DATE	THEMES
Beltane/May Day/May Eve	May 1	The renewal of the goddess, the return of spring, sexuality
Summer Solstice/ Midsummer/Litha	Approximately June 21	The longest day, the conquering sun, the waning versus waxing year
August Eve/Lammas/ Lughnasadh	August 1 or 2	First harvest, grain harvest, the sacrifice of the grain god
Fall Equinox/Mabon/ Harvest Home	Approximately September 21	Second harvest, balance of light and dark, thanksgiving
Samhain/Halloween	October 31	Final harvest, death and rebirth, the power of the god
Winter Solstice/Yule	Approximately December 21	The birth of the sun, the waxing versus waning year, light in darkness
February Eve/Candlemas/ Brigid/Imbolg/Oimelc	February 2	Preparation for spring, hope for returning warmth, milk
Spring Equinox/Ostara	Approximately March 21	Returning warmth, balance of dark and light, eggs

DIVINATION

Some form of divination—reading the future and the unknown present—has always been a part of the folk magician's trade. Once the witch and conjurer became conflated in the Middle Ages, it became as much a part of the witch's repertoire as the broomstick.

Divination helps with magic, as it can guide the purpose and direction of a spell, revealing answers about how to do the magical work. Tarot and astrology, two forms of divination used by witches, will be discussed later. Others include reading tea leaves, palmistry, reading Norse runes, and many more.

CURSES AND BANISHING

The curse is the original work of the witch, and it hasn't gone away. Some witches (usually Wiccan) are opposed to cursing of any kind, but many others say context matters. Just as the book *Aradia* allowed for poisoning those who oppress others (see page 25), some witches are comfortable with curses.

A curse or hex imposes a specified form of harm on the target. A banishing drives the target away. An evil person can be banished, but so can a disease or tumor. A binding entraps an evildoer so that they can do no harm. That said, the mildest magical way of dealing with an enemy is to bless them, turning them away from harm so that they are too happy and pleasant to make any trouble.

WITCHES, MAGIC, AND THE OCCULT

Like folk magic, witchcraft may be overlooked or taken for granted since it draws much from the natural world. This is why, historically, it both is and isn't included in the occult. However, the very act of magic is occult by definition, and witches have always incorporated occult arts and sciences into their spells, rituals, and practices.

- Modern witchcraft, including Wicca, is a direct descendant of earlier forms of occultism.
- Wicca is highly influenced by the occult revival of the nineteenth century, a rich stew of occult practices (see the timeline on page 154).
- Witches practice a variety of occult arts, including ceremonial magic, astrology, tarot, and Kabbalah.

Different covens and different solitary witches have a greater or lesser interest in other occult arts, but the connection is unmistakable.

CHAPTER 3

ASTROLOGY

The study of the stars began around 5,000 years ago in Mesopotamia to guide planting and harvesting, as well as to aid in navigation. Studying the stars (astronomy) eventually led to studying predictions from the stars, and from there, divination using the stars (astrology) was born. As we've learned, the core principle of Western occultism is "As above, so below." This means the microcosm is a reflection of the macrocosm—"As the universe, so the soul." So developing a science that connects the stars to human fate makes sense.

Western astrology began around 2,400 years ago, spreading from Babylon to Egypt and then to Greece. But astrology is not just a Western concept. China has a millennia-long history of astrology, which remains untouched by Western influence, with 12 signs each ruling a year for a cycle of 12 years. India also had its own astrology by around 1000 BCE. As you may recall from the introduction, Alexander the Great spread Greek culture all over the ancient world while absorbing other beliefs and practices. In this way, Greek and Indian (Jyotish) astrology had a lasting influence on each other.

Even though our solar system is heliocentric, with the sun at the center, astrology is geocentric: the Earth is treated as the center because we are predicting what happens *here*, whether it involves planting our crops or understanding our souls.

Imagine a sphere with the Earth at the center and the night sky projected onto it. Throughout the year, the sun traces an imaginary circle (the "ecliptic") through what astronomers call the celestial sphere. The Babylonians divided the ecliptic into twelve equal segments and named each after the biggest constellation in that segment. The Greeks called this the "zodiac" because most of the constellations were named for animals ("zo-" is the root of "zoo").

The ecliptic can be calculated two ways: sidereal and tropical. When this system of astrology was created, the resulting zodiacal map was about the same either way, regardless of the method of calculation. However, two millennia later, the natural movement of the stars means that sidereal and tropical calculations give very different results. For instance, in tropical astrology, I'm a Taurus, born between April 21 and May 21. In sidereal astrology, I'm an Aries. Tropical astrology is generally used by Western astrologers, and sidereal primarily by Jyothi astrologers.

Until the Enlightenment period, astrology was a widespread and accepted science. The rationalism of the period rejected astrology as an unenlightened pseudoscience. Between intellectual and Church opposition to astrology, a great deal of knowledge was lost. In fact, Western astrology had almost died out by the early 1900s. What then emerged became "modern" or "revival" astrology, with new ideas filling in the gaps. In a fascinating twist of events, new documents (and new translations of documents) were discovered in the late twentieth century, bringing about a revival of "traditional" astrology. We'll get more into the differences between traditional and modern astrology later on.

Today, with traditional astrology on the rise, as well as a modernist backlash, there's significant controversy between modern and traditional schools, but well-known astrologer and author Chris Brennan sees a future in which the schools are blended.

◈✦┤ MEET ├─✦◈
PTOLEMY

Claudius Ptolemy (circa 100–170 CE), an Egyptian of Greek descent, was an astronomer, astrologer, mathematician, musician, and geographer. His manual of astrology, *Tetrabiblos*, remains an influential work, applying mathematics to astrology. His Ptolemaic system of mapping the universe, which argued for a geocentric universe, was widespread throughout the ancient world.

Although we now know that the Earth is not stationary in, nor the center of, the universe, the ideas of geocentric astrology remain. Ptolemy saw astrology as scientific and argued that it was like medicine—you started with scientific fact and then drew conclusions.

WHAT IS A HOROSCOPE?

Astrology includes a lot of technical terminology and detail that can be daunting to a beginner. There are more nuances to learn in astrology than in any other occult science except alchemy. Nonetheless, a few key concepts can bring a great deal of insight. (Some will also come in handy as we discuss other occult sciences.) Keep reading to better understand the basics of astrology.

Let's start with the horoscope, which is a map of the sky at an exact moment in time. Your horoscope, or chart, is the map of the moment of your birth. Each of the components explained in the following pages appears on a horoscope, so a basic understanding of them will open a world of insight. The horoscope itself is drawn on a chart—usually circular—divided into twelve segments (see the illustration on page 38).

THE SIGNS OF THE ZODIAC

When someone asks, "What's your sign?" they're referring to one of the twelve constellations that comprise the zodiac. The Sun is in each sign (segment of the sky) for approximately the dates shown in the following table (plus or minus a day or two, year over year).

SIGN	SYMBOL	DATES	KEYWORDS
Aries	♈ The Ram	March 21–April 19	Charismatic, competitive, egoistic
Taurus	♉ The Bull	April 20–May 20	Practical, possessive, domestic
Gemini	♊ The Twins	May 21–June 20	Changeable, communicative, versatile
Cancer	♋ The Crab	June 21–July 22	Emotional, sensitive, nurturing
Leo	♌ The Lion	July 23–August 22	Proud, confident, creative
Virgo	♍ The Virgin	August 23–September 22	Careful, organized, analytical
Libra	♎ The Scales	September 23–October 22	Persuasive, fair, indecisive
Scorpio	♏ The Scorpion	October 23–November 21	Erotic, mysterious, deceptive
Sagittarius	♐ The Archer	November 22–December 21	Optimistic, wise, open
Capricorn	♑ The Goat	December 22–January 19	Cautious, perfectionist, conventional
Aquarius	♒ The Water-Bearer	January 20–February 18	Independent, inventive, unconventional
Pisces	♓ The Fish	February 19–March 20	Visionary, empathic, impractical

THE PLANETS

Because astrology is geocentric, the Earth isn't counted as a planet. But the Sun and the Moon *are* counted as "planets" (more accurately, "lights" or "luminaries"). Uranus, Neptune, and Pluto are called the outer planets because they are not visible to the naked eye. (Astrology doesn't care that Pluto was demoted to dwarf planet.) The planets and their symbols and meanings are shown in the chart below.

The date ranges for each sign in the chart on page 42 are those of the Sun sign. For example, the sun is in Aries from March 21 through April 19. But every planet is in some segment of the sky—in a sign—at any given moment. They all orbit at different rates and move from sign to sign at their own pace.

To set up a chart, you would start with an exact date, time, latitude, and longitude for whatever is being charted. This helps you define the positions of the planets and the position of the Ascendant, or Rising, sign—the sign that is rising in the east at that moment.

As mentioned, a chart is a circle with twelve segments. The Ascendant is at 180 degrees (due west), and the remaining signs are in order from there, clockwise. So if your Ascendant is Aries, then Taurus is in the next segment, and Gemini the next. The planets are then placed in the segment for the sign they're in. If your Moon is in Gemini, you would add the Moon to the Gemini segment.

PLANET	SYMBOL	MEANING IN A CHART
Sun	☉	Self, ego, energy
Moon	☽	Emotions, unconscious
Mercury	☿	Communication, intellect, language

TABLE CONTINUED ▶

PLANET	SYMBOL	MEANING IN A CHART
Venus	♀	Love, relationship, art, beauty
Mars	♂	Aggression, courage, sex, competition
Jupiter	♃	Expansion, optimism, luck
Saturn	♄	Restriction, law, responsibility
Uranus	♅	Rebellion, reformation, eccentricity
Neptune	♆	Mysticism, intuition, delusion
Pluto	♇	Transformation, death and rebirth, evolution
Ascendant	A^{sc}	Appearances

The planets are the beginning of a horoscope, forming a complex and holistic description of a person, event, or anything else being charted. My sun sign is Taurus, so I am domestic and practical, sometimes even dull. But we add nuance when we understand that my Jupiter is in Aquarius—I am most expansive and optimistic when I am unconventional.

THE HOUSES

"If a sign is the portion of sky a planet is in, the house is where that portion of sky is in relation to where you are on Earth."

—URSULA RISING, ASTROLOGER

The twelve houses are added to the chart like spokes on a wheel. The first house is at the Ascendant, and they go around counterclockwise. There are various systems for calculating the houses: Placidus, Whole Sign, and Equal are the most common, but there are many others, such as Koch, Regiomontanus, and Morinus. House systems are one of the most controversial topics in astrology, but a beginner can safely use whatever your app or website provides (see page 157).

HOUSE	MEANING
1st	Self, ego, and physical appearance. Beginnings.
2nd	Material and physical things. Physical needs. Senses. Money, acquisitions, self-esteem.
3rd	Communication, travel, education (schools, teachers), neighborhoods. Siblings. Environment.
4th	Home, foundation, privacy. Family and roots (especially mother). Children, nurturing.
5th	Fun, play, recreation. Entertainment, drama, creativity, color, romance. Fertility. Self-expression.
6th	Fitness, health, routines, duties, organization. Job. Being of service to others. Pets.
7th	Others who are significant—marriage and business partners, clients, and enemies. Contracts. Diplomacy. Agreements.

TABLE CONTINUED ▶

HOUSE	MEANING
8th	Birth, death, rebirth. Sex, transformation, mystery. Real estate, inheritance, investments: things associated with other people's money.
9th	Long-distance travel, foreign languages. Inspiration. Higher education. Law, religion, philosophy, and ethics.
10th	Society and government. Boundaries, authority. Father. Notoriety. Advantage. Ambitions, career, achievements.
11th	Friends, groups, social communities, social justice, and charity. Gifts, benefactors, hopes, and dreams.
12th	Endings, old age, the afterlife. Privacy, seclusion, and retreating. Intuition. Secrets.

The houses add another layer of nuance to the chart. My Jupiter is in Aquarius in the third house. The expansiveness, luck, and optimism of Jupiter are most present in communication and travel—perhaps this is why my writing does so well (Jupiter) and why I write (third house) on "eccentric" (Aquarius) subjects. As you can see, perceiving three components together—sign, planet, house—makes your chart unique. (House calculation can be done for you by any of the apps or websites on page 157.)

ELEMENTS AND QUALITIES

So far, we've looked at signs, planets, and houses, which together yield a total of 34 different pieces of information. Let's simplify this for a moment. Each sign is one of the four elements: Earth, Air, Fire, and Water. Elemental signs have a great deal in common with one another:

- ◆ **EARTH** is practical, physical, domestic, slow-moving, and conventional.
  - → Signs: Taurus, Virgo, and Capricorn

- ◆ **AIR** is thought, inspiration, beginnings, language, movement, and imagination.
  - → Signs: Gemini, Libra, and Aquarius

- ◆ **FIRE** is impulsive, passionate, aggressive, energetic, and intense.
  - → Signs: Aries, Leo, and Sagittarius

- ◆ **WATER** is emotional, fluid, intuitive, and dreamlike.
  - → Signs: Cancer, Scorpio, and Pisces

If you look at the descriptions for each sign, you can see how their element ties them together—Taurus is practical, Virgo is careful, and Capricorn is cautious, all Earth qualities. People often find they have natural compatibility with others of the same element.

Signs also have one of three "qualities":

- ◆ **CARDINAL** signs initiate; they lead and bring energy.
  - → Signs: Aries, Cancer, Libra, and Capricorn

- ◆ **FIXED** signs sustain; they solidify and establish.
  - → Signs: Taurus, Leo, Scorpio, and Aquarius

- ◆ **MUTABLE** signs transition; they adapt and change, move, and can destroy.
  - → Signs: Gemini, Virgo, Sagittarius, and Pisces

As you see, each sign has a unique combination of element and quality.

GETTING STARTED IN ASTROLOGY

Astrology is a science for those who love to read, study, and test theories. To start, you'll need a few things:

BEGINNER BOOKS. Try *Astrology* by Carole Taylor or *Astrology for Yourself* by Demetra George and Douglas Bloch.

SOFTWARE FOR DRAWING CHARTS AND LOOKING UP OTHER INFORMATION. I love the website Astro.com and the app TimePassages.

YOUR OWN EXACT TIME AND PLACE OF BIRTH. If you don't have it, you can arrange to purchase a detailed, long-form birth certificate. This is needed for an accurate birth chart. The Ascendant changes about every two hours, and your entire chart is based on the position of the Ascendant.

A DIARY, such as the annual *Llewellyn's Daily Planetary Guide*. Get in the habit of writing down major events of the day to compare your book-learning with real experience. Often, as she was learning astrology, my daughter, Ursula Rising, would ask questions like, "Mom, what happened in June 1996?" She compared dates that were supposed to be significant, according to her studies, with empirical evidence. If you can get birth times for some friends and cooperate together on asking these kinds of questions, all the better.

PLANETS, ELEMENTS, QUALITIES

In a chart, we'll see the symbols for the planets in their houses, with a bunch of lines between them (we'll get to those soon). It's a lot to take in at once. However, it can be helpful to get a feel for a chart by looking at the distribution of the planets.

YOU'LL NEED:

Pen/pencil and notepad   Chart-drawing tool (see page 157)

INSTRUCTIONS:

1. Create a natal (birth) chart by entering the date, time, and place of your birth into your chart-drawing tool. If you don't know what time you were born, use noon (the most common birthtime in the United States), but for the most accuracy, track down this information, if possible.

2. Notice that each planet lands in a sign. Record the planet and sign in two columns. For example:

PLANET	SIGN
Sun	Capricorn
Moon	Cancer
Mercury	Capricorn
Venus	Aquarius
Mars	Sagittarius
Jupiter	Cancer

TABLE CONTINUED ▶

PLANETS, ELEMENTS, QUALITIES CONTINUED

PLANET	SIGN
Saturn	Capricorn
Uranus	Capricorn
Neptune	Capricorn
Pluto	Scorpio
Ascendant	Scorpio

3. Add two more columns, one for the element and one for the quality of each sign (see page 47). Continuing with the example:

PLANET	SIGN	ELEMENT	QUALITY
Sun	Capricorn	Earth	Cardinal
Moon	Cancer	Water	Cardinal
Mercury	Capricorn	Earth	Cardinal
Venus	Aquarius	Air	Fixed
Mars	Sagittarius	Fire	Mutable
Jupiter	Cancer	Water	Cardinal
Saturn	Capricorn	Earth	Cardinal
Uranus	Capricorn	Earth	Cardinal
Neptune	Capricorn	Earth	Cardinal
Pluto	Scorpio	Water	Fixed
Ascendant	Scorpio	Water	Fixed

4. Count the elements and qualities in the chart from step 3 and make a distribution chart like this:

Earth	5
Air	1
Fire	1
Water	4
Cardinal	7
Fixed	3
Mutable	1

5. Now it's up to you to read the chart: What do you know about this person *just* from this information? What does a preponderance of one element or quality tell you about this person's strengths and weaknesses? Don't forget to read the absences! Sometimes a person has none of an element or quality. What would that mean? The person in this example is Earthy and very Cardinal—what does that mean? These are questions to ponder as you learn more.

The Aspects of Angles

The relationship *between* planets creates harmonies and tensions, and here we start to see impact on events. Any two planets on a chart form angles, and some of these angles are known as "aspects." Ptolemy explained that the way the circle is divided represents the divisions of octaves in music. Thus, harmony and disharmony are not merely metaphors, but representations of the "music" of the planets.

Here are the major aspects:

ASPECT	SYMBOL	DEGREE/ POSITION	DESCRIPTION
Conjunct	☌	0° (in the same sign)	United; these planets have energies that blend; they can be harmonious or a blind spot.
Opposite	☍	180° (directly across from each other)	Disharmonious, but the tension created is often toward a positive outcome; these two planets push and motivate each other.
Square	☐	90° (right angle; 3 signs apart)	Disharmonious and blocking; these two planets are at cross-purposes and tend to block each other's energies.

ASPECT	SYMBOL	DEGREE/POSITION	DESCRIPTION
Trine	△	120° (4 signs apart)	Harmonious; the planets work together and enrich each other; trines show natural talents and ease.
Sextile	✳	60° (2 signs apart)	Harmonious; tends to show more noticeable talents; energies that can be directed.

When you look at a chart, the lines drawn show the aspects; often, charts show harmonies and disharmonies in different colors. Charts also show aspects to your Ascendant and your Midheaven (the point at the very top of the chart).

Earlier, I noted that my Sun is in Taurus, but my Jupiter is in Aquarius. These planets are "square"; they tend to block each other. My expansiveness (Jupiter) gets pushed aside by my sense of who I am (Sun). You could say one of my tasks in life is to figure out how to stop blocking Jupiter from helping me. On the other hand, with Sun conjunct Mercury, and both trine the Moon, I can easily accept my emotions as a part of who I am, and communicating comes naturally to me.

You can read a chart's overall trends: lots of squares and oppositions, or lots of trines and sextiles, indicate a hard or an easy life, respectively. Concentrate on the inner planets (Sun, Moon, Mercury, Mars, and Venus), which provide more practical information about love, work, and family.

TYPES OF ASTROLOGY

As mentioned, Western astrology is currently split between modern and traditional practices, each of which have a few subsets. Jyotish astrology, rooted in India, has significant overlap with Western astrology, as well as many differences. And Chinese astrology is a whole different animal. Let's dive in.

MODERN WESTERN ASTROLOGY

Many of the distinctions between modern and traditional astrology are technical, but some are easily understood. Modern astrology is more focused on a person's character, emotions, behaviors, and relationships. It uses the outer planets (Uranus, Neptune, and Pluto) and newer developments in the field, such as asteroids. The purpose of modern astrology is seen as an examination of the soul, and it tends toward optimism, allowing for free will overcoming the destiny seen in the stars. There are a number of specialized schools of thought:

EVOLUTIONARY OR KARMIC ASTROLOGY places a heavy emphasis on the planet Pluto. It works to track the soul's journey from lifetime to lifetime.

URANIAN ASTROLOGY, developed by Alfred Witte, is a completely different method of horoscope creation, using different math and aiming for more precision, especially in prediction.

PSYCHOLOGICAL ASTROLOGY is one of the major offshoots of modern astrology—its greatest twentieth-century innovation. This field is deeply influenced by the theories of Carl Jung. Jung, a pioneer in psychiatry and psychoanalysis and a contemporary of Sigmund Freud, was fascinated by the occult, and he explored alchemy and tarot as well as astrology. Jung even used horoscopes as part of analysis. Psychological astrology sees the purpose of astrology as deepening one's understanding of oneself. Essentially, your horoscope reflects your soul, your opportunities, and your challenges.

◇→— MEET —←◇
EVANGELINE ADAMS

Evangeline Adams (1868–1932) was a popular astrologer with an upscale clientele that included the Prince of Wales and J. P. Morgan. She was arrested three times in New York City for practicing astrology (which was illegal at the time). In 1914, a judge gave her an anonymous chart to read, and she accurately described the judge's son with such detail that he freed her, saying, "Adams raises astrology to the dignity of an exact science."

Occultist Aleister Crowley (see page 128) ghostwrote for Adams, and she ghostwrote for him as well, at minimum "contributing" to his book *The General Principles of Astrology*. She married a much younger man, may have had an affair with Crowley, and was a "companion" to actress Emma Viola Sheridan Fry until her death.

TRADITIONAL WESTERN ASTROLOGY

The traditional rebirth is the most significant twenty-first-century trend in astrology. It places a greater emphasis on a person's fate and on external events. It uses astrology in more structured ways and has more complex and specific predictive techniques.

The schools of traditional astrology are named after the time period and place from which their recovered documents originate— for example, Hellenistic, Renaissance, and Medieval. However, they all have much more in common with one another than with any modern form; indeed, more than modern forms have with one another. Let's take a look:

HELLENISTIC ASTROLOGY is the most popular traditional form. Like all traditional astrology, it uses only the seven visible planets. It was during the Hellenic period that astrology as we know it today came about, marrying the house system of the Egyptians with the zodiac of Mesopotamia. The "four-fold system" of signs, planets, houses, and aspects was thus born, and it is still used today. Hellenistic astrology uses techniques previously lost, including "sects," which distinguish between daytime and nighttime charts, and "time lord" techniques, which allow pinpoint predictions of events in a person's life.

RENAISSANCE AND MEDIEVAL ASTROLOGY use the grimoires of such mages as Agrippa (see page 79). They differ primarily in the authors they cite (Renaissance draws particularly on William Lilly; see page 58). Both work astrological magic and create astrological talismans as part of their tradition.

CHINESE ASTROLOGY

Chinese astrology (*Sheng Xiao*, or "born resembling") has 12 zodiacal animals that repeat in a 12-year, rather than 1-year, cycle. Each year also has a Chinese element—unlike in the Western system, there are five: Metal, Water, Wood, Fire, and Earth. Thus, there's actually a 60-year cycle before each unique combination of element and animal repeats. That is, if you were born in 2010, you are a metal tiger, but if you were born in 1974, you are a wood tiger. See page 157 for a few websites where you can look up your Chinese animal and element by birth year.

Most people in the West are familiar with Chinese astrology based on the lunar calendar, with one animal per year, but feng shui astrology allows for the astrological calculation of an hour, day, and month as well.

Jyotish Astrology

Jyotish ("science of light" in Sanskrit) is a tradition from India that emphasizes a lineage of teachers. It uses the sidereal zodiac (see page 40). Also known as Jyotisha, Hindu astrology, or Vedic astrology, it considers your sign to be your Ascendent, not your Sun sign. Jyotish never underwent a period of suppression and is widely accepted in India. For example, Indian matchmaking still relies heavily on compatibility charts for prospective couples.

HOW ASTROLOGY IS USED

A horoscope can be used in many ways, since two charts can interact with each other, and a chart can interact with the present moment. "Transits," or the movement of planets across the sky (and therefore across the chart), allow for predictions about the present and future. When two charts are read together, they have aspects, just as one chart does, which can provide insight into relationships. In addition to the common practices outlined in the following section, there are also medical astrology, magical and talismanic astrology, geomancy, and many more disciplines, each with a specific, practical purpose.

Predictive Astrology

The most familiar type of astrology is what you'd see in the newspaper: the forecast for your day. Predictive astrology looks at the interaction between significant transits and a horoscope. Using only a Sun sign (as the newspaper does) gives limited information, but looking at today's transits on an astrology website, I see that my Mars is sextile Mars for a few days, giving me vigor, health, and energy. Whether it's predicting today or the coming year, this type of astrology is probably the most commonly sought by the public.

Electional Astrology

Almost every astrologer uses electional astrology to determine the best timing for important events. Wedding dates, contract signings, opening a business—all can be elected to the minute for the best possible future. In some cases, you are selecting the most auspicious transits, such as choosing the best date to have surgery. In other cases, you're selecting the ideal birth date and time—your marriage or new business will have its own chart, calculating from the day it's "born."

Horary Astrology

Horary astrology is a highly specialized practice from traditional astrology that answers specific questions through chart-reading. The exact time the question is asked, plus a highly structured set of interpretations of the houses, is used to answer virtually anything—often quite practical, mundane questions, such as the location of a lost object.

◇→┤ MEET ├←◇
WILLIAM LILLY

William Lilly (1602–1681) was considered the most important astrologer in England. He was the author of *Christian Astrology*, a massive tome and the first of its kind in English (rather than the customary Latin). This book is a classic of traditional astrology, and one of the foremost texts on horary astrology—it has never gone out of print.

The son of a farmer, Lilly married a wealthy widow and used his life of leisure to study astrology in depth. In the last year of his life, he wrote an autobiography, *William Lilly's History of His Life and Times*, which includes biographical portraits of famed magicians John Dee and Edward Kelley.

SYNASTRY ASTROLOGY

Synastry is the astrology of relationships. It is used to determine the compatibility and potential success of a relationship, whether romantic, business, or any other, by overlaying two charts. The position of each person's Venus in relation to the other person's planets is particularly significant. It becomes quite intricate, and special kinds of chart-drawing are used.

GEOGRAPHIC ASTROLOGY

Also known as astrocartography or locational or relocation astrology, this discipline overlays significant chart lines on a map to determine what places have resonance, good fortune, and disharmony for you. With your birthplace as a center point, a personalized map is created and interpreted by an astrologer trained in this specialty.

ASTROLOGY IN THE OCCULT

Hermes Trismegistus called astrology one of the "three parts of wisdom." As an astrologer himself, he knew that because "that which is above is like that which is below," the stars are reflected in human life. The other two parts of wisdom are alchemy and magic. As we can see, these great occult arts are interconnected.

- Heinrich Cornelius Agrippa, author of *Three Books of Occult Philosophy*, was also an astrologer, and like Hermes Trismegistus, is still studied by occultists. Agrippa knew that studying the stars was key to occult philosophy.
- Astrology depends on an understanding of the four elements (see page 47), which permeate Western occultism. The elements are key to ceremonial magic, Kabbalah, tarot, and alchemy, and they are a part of Wicca as well.
- Astrology also depends on a study of the planets, and these, too, are crucial in magic and alchemy. The number order of the signs and the numbers of the houses connect to numerology; each aspect of the occult is connected to a bigger picture.

The astrological map of the universe, and its component understanding, simply permeates occultism. You don't have to be an astrologer to be an occultist (I'm definitely not), but its principles must be understood. If you understand Earth signs, you can understand Earth magic, Earth meditation, and so on. Astrology makes you a better occultist—and the occult makes you a better astrologer.

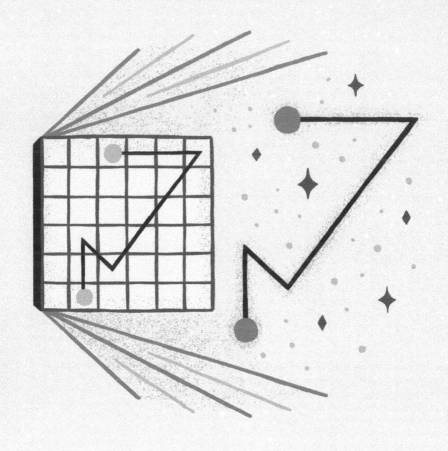

CHAPTER 4

NUMEROLOGY

Numbers have been used since humans first began thinking in a symbolic way, and numerology—the study of the occult meaning of numbers—has existed since we first started thinking magically. Basically, numerology has been around forever. To quote Carl Jung, "A mathematician once remarked that everything in science was man-made except numbers, which had been created by God himself."

While many numerology systems sometimes contradict one another, they also share some basic truths. For the most part, numerological systems are a Western phenomenon, arising in Greece and the Middle East. In other cultures, such as in China and Japan, there are traditions associated with lucky and unlucky numbers, but not systematic readings, personality analysis, or numeric magic.

The oldest numerological system is known as Chaldean numerology, although it may have arisen in Mesopotamia *before* the Chaldean civilization (circa 600 BCE). It ascribes an energetic value to each number and corresponds letters to numbers. Thus, names, words, and dates can all have numerological meaning. Pythagoras also created his eponymous numerological system around 600 BCE in Greece. We'll discuss both systems in this chapter.

The early Church banned numerology, along with astrology and other forms of occultism. Nevertheless, there are numbers of power in Christianity—such as 888, the "Jesus number," and 666, the "number of the Beast." Some forms of Christian numerology persist today, especially in the Eastern Orthodox Church.

Judaism has its own numerological system, too. Every letter in the Hebrew alphabet has a numeric value, so every word can be totaled up. Gematria is the mystical art of finding hidden meanings in the Bible by relating words to one another if they come to the same total. A famous example is in Genesis: Abraham is said to have 318 men who defeat an army, but his servant's name, Eliezer, equals 318, suggesting perhaps that Eliezer alone helped Abraham.

The earliest known use of gematria is a tomb dating to about 700 BCE. The rabbinic use dates to about 200 CE. Gematria is essential to Kabbalah (we will learn more about this in chapter 6). The oldest Jewish mystical text, the *Sefer Yetzirah*, elaborates the meaning of each letter/number in the creation of the universe.

During the Renaissance, a whole new kind of numeric magic was born. It dates at least to 1440, but is best known from Agrippa's *Three Books of Occult Philosophy*, first printed in 1531. This is the "planetary number square," and such squares are still in use by ceremonial magicians.

Another important numerological text of around the same period was *The Garden of Cyrus, or The Quincuncial Lozenge* by Sir Thomas Browne. It is focused entirely on the number five and the "quincunx pattern." This pattern is five dots—four in a square and one in the center, such as found on dice. Browne believed the quincunx showed a mystical connection between art and nature.

In the twentieth century, Carl Jung was fascinated by the mystical properties of numbers. Though Jung claimed to hate math, the numbers themselves, he felt, touched upon divinity. His work may well be responsible for the popularity of numerology today.

Today, Pythagorean and Chaldean are the numerological systems most commonly used. Although some occultists use them, they are primarily the province of the New Age movement. To be fair, it's hard to define "New Age," so the dividing line from occultism isn't always clear, but New Age tends more toward a blending of Eastern and Western systems, is more holistic and wellness-oriented, and relies heavily on new or emerging understandings of esoteric systems. It is also decidedly "lighter," eschewing anything that seems spooky and almost completely avoiding actual magic. The New Age movement employs numerology far more often than occultists do. Nevertheless, numerology is an occult practice, so let's give it a closer look.

MATH IS MAGIC

There is a long history of mathematicians who were also mystics; Pythagoras and Isaac Newton were not anomalies. Math shows an underlying pattern to all things. There are repetitions and rhythms throughout nature and the cosmos. This sense of harmony may also explain why so many mathematicians are also musicians, including Albert Einstein.

Math also touches infinity. For example, pi is the ratio of a circle's circumference to its diameter, most commonly represented as 3.14. Many numbers can be said to have infinite decimal places—1/3 is .333, with no number of threes that is perfectly accurate. Pi, though, has infinite digits with no pattern. It has been calculated, per *Guinness World Records*, to over 50 trillion places.

Imagining that can blow your mind—an infinite string of threes, an infinite string of pi, flowing past all human and natural confines—anyone who contemplates such things can easily become mystical. Occultism, which deals in both underlying patterns and mind-blowing concepts, is a natural place for numbers.

◇→⊢ MEET ⊢→◇
PYTHAGORAS

Pythagoras of Samos (circa 570–495 BCE) was a Greek
philosopher who influenced Plato, Aristotle, and Western
occultism, as well as mathematics and philosophy in general. He is the subject of endless speculation, because none
of his writings survive, so we have only documents written
about him. We know that he founded a school based on
his philosophy in Southern Italy, where initiates were
vegetarians and lived communally.

He is credited with coining the word "philosophy" (love
of knowledge); determining that the morning and evening
stars were the planet Venus; breakthroughs in mathematics, including the Pythagorean theorem; and much more.

◇◇◇

NUMBERS AS UNDERLYING TRUTH

Beyond arithmetic or sequences, there are some universal things
about numbers most of us understand. For example, you know that
one is singular, alone, independent. This may give you thoughts of
singular people, such as leaders: There are lots of people, but only
one leader. One is the "alpha." Two probably reminds you of couples, relationships, and connections.

Notice how these descriptions correspond to the first two
signs of the zodiac: Aries, the first sign, is a leader, and Taurus, the
second, is ruled by Venus and deeply concerned with relationships.
This isn't a coincidence—numbers reflect underlying truths, and
their meaning resonates throughout the occult.

Traditions of numerology interpret a number's truth in
different ways. The higher the number, the more variety in interpretation. People are generally going to agree about one, two, three,
and four—numbers with distinct natures that all of us see in life.

Numbers as Building Blocks

For numbers to be interpreted, they have to be a part of something. The variations of numerology in this chapter correspond letters to numbers, so that numbers become the building blocks of names and other words. However, each numerology system originated in connection with an alphabet other than Latin (English), so the translation into English isn't perfect. (Pythagoras was Greek, gematria is Hebrew, and Aramaic was the language of Chaldea.)

Similarly, numbers are the building blocks of dates, but different calendrical systems exist. For example, I was born in May, which is the fifth month of the Gregorian calendar, but in the Hebrew calendar, I was born in the sixth month, Iyar.

The idea in any of these systems is that numbers have an inherent resonance that can transcend such limitations. Astrology only works if the moment of your birth is no accident, but connects with the stars at that exact time. Similarly, your name and date of birth in numerology are understood to have a resonance that connects you to these numbers.

Understanding numbers as building blocks leads us to realize that we can make conscious choices about numbers—imprinting a number's energy into something purposely, as we'll see on page 80.

Magical Geometry and Measurement

So far, we've talked about numbers as themselves and numbers as corresponding to letters, words, and dates. But this leaves out one of the most important uses of numbers: measurement.

Freemasonry, a magical lodge tradition, places spiritual and mystical significance on the Craft of masonry. Their symbols—the compass and the square—represent the careful measurement and construction performed by a working mason, as well as the allegorical "straightness" and "trueness" that are Masonic values.

Medieval European churches were built in accordance with specific geometric rules; supposedly not just rules of architecture, but spiritual and magical principles—mathematical relationships that create resonance. Anyone who's visited a medieval basilica has felt a magical "something" standing in certain parts of the church. The geometry creates nexuses of power. This resonance was once part of Freemasonry's deepest magical teachings.

The other use of magical measurement is in tools and structures used in magic. Some ceremonial magic, and some traditions of Wicca, require certain tools to be measured exactly. So, for example, one Wiccan tradition might say that a wand is a carved piece of wood, but another might prescribe an exact length for that wand. The same might be true of the circumference of the magic circle, the pentacle, or other tools. The idea, again, is that the measurement itself is creating resonance and power that will become a part of the rite in which the tool is used.

VARIETIES OF NUMEROLOGY

"Numerology" simply means that numbers have magical, spiritual, symbolic, or other occult properties. There's a wide variety of customs and rituals surrounding numbers in different cultures. For example, most Indigenous American Sun Dance ceremonies emphasize the number four, representing the temporal world—there are four poles in the ceremonial tipi, and durations and repetitions in multiples of four. In China, four is deeply unlucky, the way thirteen is in the US, and similarly, some buildings do not have a fourth floor.

Such number magic is seen in meaningful numerical repetitions, in choosing dates for important events, in the construction of buildings and items, and in the number of letters in a name. Since numerology can include corresponding numbers to letters, "numerology" can be about words as well as numbers. Or numerology might refer to the use of math or measurement for a magical result. Finally, numerology can also be systems of correspondences, finding meaning in words (especially names) and dates. This is what most people think of as numerology, even though it's the least-common sort. Let's take a closer look at this mixed bag.

CHALDEAN NUMEROLOGY

Chaldean numerology is still in use today, somewhat in the West, but mostly by Indian numerologists. This system corresponds the numbers one through eight to the letters of the alphabet. Correspondences are based on the *sound* of letters (or their "vibration"). The number nine is not used in letter correspondences because it is considered sacred and tied to infinity. Chaldean numerology is a predictive divination system—showing your life path and destiny.

Single-digit correspondences are shown in the table on page 70, which is typical but not definitive; there is a wide variation of interpretations according to different sources. If you're interested in studying this system in depth, you'll also want the meanings for the two-digit numbers, called compound numbers (see page 157).

When interpreting a name in Chaldean numerology, your "vibration" is considered to be your commonly used name. For instance, if your name is Robert, but everyone calls you Bob, you'd interpret Bob.

NUMBER	LETTERS	PLANET	MEANINGS
1	A, Q, Y, I, J	Sun	Freedom, independence, ambition, hedonism, leadership, self-reliance
2	B, R, K	Moon	Adaptability, weakness, melancholy, creativity, empathy
3	G, C, L, S	Jupiter	Expansion, growth, knowledge, strategy
4	D, M, T	Uranus	Inventive, science, anti-authority, revolutionary, discipline
5	E, H, N, X	Mercury	Communication, social, movement, friends, business, travel
6	U, V, W	Venus	Receptive, comfort, charming, stubborn
7	O, Z	Neptune	The shadow of two, insight, intuition, intelligent, curious
8	F, P	Saturn	The destiny number, determination, ambition, money, cynical, pragmatic
9		Mars and Pluto	The divine

✧→⊢ MEET ⊢←✧
CHEIRO

"Cheiro" (1866–1936), born William John Warner, and also
known as Count Louis Hamon, was the author of *Cheiro's
Book of Numbers,* which remains the most influential work
on Chaldean numerology. Cheiro was an astrologer, palmist, and novelist, as well as a numerologist, and was most
famed for palm reading.

Born in Dublin, Ireland, he claimed to have learned
numerology while in India, although some have cast doubt
on this story. Cheiro traveled throughout Europe and the
United States, reading the palms of famous people, including Mark Twain, Thomas Edison, and Grover Cleveland.

◇◇

PYTHAGOREAN NUMEROLOGY

Pythagorean numerology is the most commonly used system, especially in the West, for prediction and life reading. It corresponds the
letters to the digits one through nine and uses the full name given
at birth. Pythagoras saw a relationship between musical sound and
numbers, and so found a "vibration" in numbers (similar to the
Chaldean system). However, letter correspondences move through
the alphabet in the order of the letters, rather than being based on
the sounds the letters make.

This system also uses "master numbers": 11, 22, and 33. The
master numbers are the main two-digit numbers read in this
system, as described on page 69. The chart on pages 72 and 73
shows the Pythagorean correspondences.

NUMBER	LETTERS	PLANET	MEANINGS
1	A, J, S	Sun	Leadership, beginning, strength, independence, courage, self-sufficiency, egotism, ambition, dominance, selfish
2	B, K, T	Moon	Partnership, diplomacy, gentle, charm, supportive, relationship, cooperation, timid
3	C, L, U	Venus	Optimism, creative, social, spontaneous, imaginative, lazy, communicator, artistic
4	D, M, V	Saturn and Uranus	Practical, determined, builder, doer, traditional, security, earthy, poor health
5	E, N, W	Mercury	Progress, freedom, adventure, sensual, curious, resourceful, procrastination, aimlessness
6	F, O, X	Jupiter	Service, domestic, careful, teacher, reliable, unselfish, nervous
7	G, P, Y	Neptune	Investigator, loner, eccentric, analysis, inner exploration, rigid, spirituality

NUMBER	LETTERS	PLANET	MEANINGS
8	H, Q, Z	Saturn	Power, control, strength, problem-solving, money, organizer, judge, impatient, vanity
9	I, R	Mars	Universe, generalist, teacher, humanitarian, healer, old soul, occult, generosity, moody
11		Neptune	Intuition, inspiration, prophecy, nervous, impractical
22		Uranus	Materialism, spiritual mastery, negative magic
33			Spiritual, need for guidance, honesty, transformation

To begin using numerology, you need only two things: **A LETTER-TO-NUMBER CHART** and an **UNDERSTANDING OF ARITHMETIC REDUCTION**. (A third tool, a **CALCULATOR**, definitely doesn't hurt.)

I've offered a Chaldean chart (see page 70) and a Pythagorean chart (see page 72). The systems are different, and as you work with *any* system (not just numerology), you begin to bind with it; it becomes part of your deep mind. You should experiment enough with each to decide which you like and stick with exactly one system. (Don't use Hebrew numerology with a Latin alphabet, as gematria is tied to the sacredness of the Hebrew letters themselves.)

Arithmetic reduction is easiest to teach by example, so we'll start with my name, Deborah. In Pythagorean numerology, D=4, E=5, B=2, O=6, R=9, A=1, H=8. So you add these numbers together: 4+5+2+6+9+1+8=35. Recursive reduction means that you continue this process until you reach either a single digit or one of the master numbers (11, 22, or 33), which are not reduced. So we would reduce the sum 35 further: 3+5=8. My name number is 8. Now I can analyze the number 8 to learn more about myself. But keep in mind that this is only scratching the surface.

HEBREW NUMEROLOGY

Hebrew letters are numbers, just as some Latin letters are Roman numerals. The use of these numbers is the core of gematria. The number/letter connection is meaningful in Hebrew; there are several "lucky numbers," especially the number 18. Life is considered the core value of Judaism, and the word *chai* means life. Spelled חי, *chai* totals 18. Thus, Jews give gifts of $18, or $180, or another multiple of the number 18, so that life is affirmed with the gift. Each Hebrew letter also has a spiritual meaning and is part of the creation of the universe. The shape and sound of each letter, as well as its number, are a core part of Jewish mysticism.

Kabbalistic Numerology

The Hermetic Kabbalah (see page 112) uses a numerology that can be understood as Hebrew (since the Kabbalah originates in Judaism and in the Hebrew language) but is vastly simpler. In essence, each of the 10 spheres (*sephirot*) of the Tree of Life has a complex meaning, and the numbers 1 through 10 can be used to access that meaning. The 22 paths between the spheres are also numbered, and those numbers, too, can be used in magic, but it is not as common.

Chinese Numerology

Chinese numerology is not a system of correspondences, but a series of beliefs about the power of numbers for good or ill. It is based on homophones—if a word sounds like a number, that word's meaning becomes connected to the number. For example, the number six is a good number for business because it sounds like the words for "slick" in Mandarin and "happiness" in Cantonese.

Although many Chinese people speak Cantonese or another language, most number beliefs are based on Mandarin. Numbers are important culturally, and gift-giving, dates, and even decor can be connected to choosing auspicious numbers. Monetary gifts are often fortunate numbers such as 88 or 99.

USING NUMEROLOGY

Numerology is among the most practical of occult arts. We've been talking about *using* numerology from the beginning. Sure, some people will meditate on numbers (and be blown away by them), but inherently, numbers are *used*. Dates and names are chosen; some occultists have even gotten their towns to change their street addresses. (This is extreme—we'll get to simple tricks for things like street addresses later.) Things are counted, things are measured—numbers are in constant use, so much so that it's almost impossible to describe numerology without getting into the practical aspects.

LIFE PATH, DESTINY, AND PERSONALITY READINGS

On page 74, I reduced my name to the number eight using Pythagorean numerology, and it then becomes my "destiny" or "personality" number. Further research would expand our understanding of 8, and of 35—its source, in my case.

If you change your name in life, you can read the before and after names and see how your destiny has changed. This might have happened because you got married, transitioned, or took a religious name. If an occultist chooses a new name, they'll often analyze the numerology of the name before settling on it.

The "life path" or "inner talent" number is derived from one's date of birth. The life path teaches you who you are, and the destiny teaches your fate.

YOUR LIFE PATH NUMBER

In this exercise, you'll find your Pythagorean life path number using your date of birth. This number represents your inner talents, abilities, and the lessons you are to learn in life.

YOU'LL NEED:

Paper/pen and notepad   Your date of birth

INSTRUCTIONS:

1. Write down your date of birth in numeric form. For example, March 24, 1984, is 3-24-1984.

2. Reduce each number individually, as in this example. Note that the number 22 is a master number: we don't reduce it.

3	24	1984
3	2+4	1+9+8+4
3	6	22

3. Now we add the individual sums together: 3+6+22=31 and reduce 31: 3+1=4. For this reading, you would interpret the 3, the 6, the 22, and the final 4 each as a part of the destiny.

4. Looking back at the Pythagorean correspondences on page 72, for 3 we see optimism, creativity, and spontaneity. For 6, service and unselfishness. Since 3 is a communicator and 6 is a teacher, perhaps you communicate as part of teaching others. The master number 22 can represent spiritual mastery or profound negativity—a deep challenge to the service of 6 and the openness of 3. The final number, 4, is practical and solid. It can ground the negativity of 22 and allow spirituality to flourish. Thus, we see the talents and the challenges laid out in these numbers.

What do you see when you use your own birth date?

MAGIC NUMBER SQUARES

Most people consider magic number squares a math game, not occult. They are squares with whole numbers in each cell. Each row, column, and diagonal has the same sum. The first recorded number square is called the Lo Shu square and dates from the fourth-century BCE in China. It totals fifteen. This is what it looks like:

2	7	6
9	5	1
4	3	8

Renaissance grimoires assigned such "magic" squares to the planets (including the Lo Shu square, which is the square of Saturn). Agrippa spelled this out in detail, and his system is still in use. Each planetary square can be used as a talisman, amulet, or invocation of the planetary energies. The square is generally engraved into the metal that corresponds to that planet (see page 83), but you can use paper. A square can be used with or without a sigil (a sign or symbol). Sigils are of the planetary character, its intelligence, and its spirit. Such a sigil is sometimes called a "kamea." (You'll see the plural "kameas," but since it is a Hebrew word, the proper plural is "kameot," just as the plural of "sephirah" is "sephirot.")

The method of creating a kamea of a spirit or intelligence is to draw the Hebrew name of the Kabbalistic spirit assigned to the planet onto the square. First, write the name of the planetary spirit in Hebrew. Then get the number correspondence for each letter. Then spell the name by drawing a continuous line from number to number in the square for that planet, starting and ending with a circle. This line forms the invoking sigil. Page 62 shows Nachiel, the planetary intelligence of the Sun.

Magic number squares and their associated sigils are used in ceremonial magic. They are crafted into protective items (amulets) or to invoke the power of the planet or entity (talismans or tools). Some planetary spirits have a negative nature and are invoked to bring harm, so be careful to make sure you understand exactly the magic you're creating when working with these powerful symbols.

✦✦— MEET —✦✦
HEINRICH CORNELIUS AGRIPPA

Heinrich Cornelius Agrippa (1486–1535), the influential German occultist, physician, theologian, and writer, could easily be featured in half or more of the chapters of this book. His work in the occult was wide-ranging, and the influence of his *Three Books of Occult Philosophy* remains profound.

As a young man, he traveled as a mercenary soldier and was knighted by the Holy Roman Emperor. In a short span, he began writing and lecturing, received a doctorate in theology, and was denounced as a heretic, in part because he was influenced by Jews. Today, his work is studied by Hermeticists, alchemists, and magicians.

NUMEROLOGY AS A PART OF MAGIC

There are any number of approaches to using numerology in magic. Basically, you figure out how to embed any number resonances you want into *any* spell or working. I recommend you choose at most three numbers to embed (preferably one or two) and layer those numbers throughout the spell. Look at places in your work where numbers already exist and choose a specific number to create the desired resonance. Here are some considerations:

- ◆ What are the day, date, and time you are performing the magic?
- ◆ How often are you repeating the working?
- ◆ Is there a chant or incantation? How many words are in it? How many times is it repeated?
- ◆ Are you using candles? How many?
- ◆ Are you using herbs? How many?

As you can see, there are lots of ways to layer numbers and the power of numbers into any act of magic.

USING NUMBERS TO CREATE CHANGE

Numbers permeate your life. As we've seen, they can also impose energy on your life. There are certain numbers you're stuck with, ranging from your date of birth to your Social Security number. However, there are other numbers that you can manipulate.

Is there a number painted or attached to the front of your home? With a piece of chalk, you can lightly add a digit to your address, making it come to a total that creates a resonance you want in your life (just be sure it is light enough that people won't be confused by your address when making deliveries to or visiting your home!). Chalk will fade over time, so you can put the number back—or bring a new resonance in, if desired.

If your name energy is extremely difficult, you can change your name or the spelling of your name to change the energy. Depending on your surname, one or the other spelling might be more helpful to you. For example, the name Michele is sometimes spelled with two Ls, sometimes with one: Michele = 1 and Michelle = 4.

NUMEROLOGY IN THE OCCULT

Everywhere you look in the occult, there are numbers. In each of the topics we've already discussed, numerology plays a part:

- The practices of Chinese numerology (choosing lucky numbers and quantities) are fundamentally folk magic.
- The "Adding Numbers to Magic" exercise (see page 116) uses numerology within witchcraft.
- Numbers are everywhere in astrology: the numbered houses, the order of the signs as they progress through the zodiac, and the number correspondences of the planets.

This will continue through each of the occult arts we explore. Already, we've seen that Kabbalah has a powerful numerological component, and magical squares are used in ceremonial magic. Planetary and astrological numbers will play a part in alchemy, and of course, tarot cards each have a number. These numbers also cross-connect—the tarot numbers correspond to Kabbalah, the alchemical numbers are connected to astrology, and so on. As you continue to explore the occult, allow yourself to observe the presence of numbers everywhere.

CHAPTER 5

ALCHEMY

Alchemy is transformation. It is perhaps the least understood occult science, so it helps to remember this simple definition.

This ancient science—dating to Hellenized Egypt, circa 300 BCE—had four goals. First, creation of a universal solvent, called the "alkahest." Second, creation of the "panacea," an elixir for prolonged or eternal life. Next, and most famously, "substantial transmutation," turning one substance into another, typically a "base" metal (copper, lead, iron, or tin) into a "noble" metal (silver, gold, or mercury). The work of transmutation often focused on seeking the Philosopher's Stone, a theoretical substance that both was the panacea and could turn any metal into gold. The fourth goal is not discussed by modern alchemists: creation of the "homun-culus," or artificial life. In Mary Shelley's *Frankenstein*, Victor Frankenstein studies Heinrich Cornelius Agrippa and other alchemists in his quest to create his famous monster.

I have referred to alchemy as a science. It is regarded today as a pseudoscience, but the early alchemists performed tightly controlled experiments and carefully recorded their results. Alchemists also invented laboratory equipment and methods that are used to this day.

Alchemy grew out of other occult sciences and philoso-phies. Its workings were timed using astrology, and the seven metals of alchemy—gold, silver, mercury, copper, lead, iron, and tin—correspond to the astrological planets. Like astrology, alchemy follows Aristotle's physical theory: that our world is made up entirely of Earth, Air, Fire, and Water.

Alchemy initially followed the sulfur-mercury theory, which stated that metals form in the Earth when sulfur and mercury are combined. Each metal's mix of the two is unique; the more sulfur, the more spiritual the metal; the more mercury, the earthier. The "perfect" mix would yield gold. Sulfur is thought to be male and active, while mercury is female and passive. The ninth-century Arabic alchemist Jabir ibn Hayyan (also known as Geber), sometimes called the father of chemistry, was among the most famous proponents of this theory. Much later, Paracelsus (see page 85) changed this polarity into a trinity. In 1530, he published *Opus Paramirum*, which defined the "three primes" of sulfur, mercury, and salt.

It's a misconception that chemistry "evolved" from alchemy. Rather, chemistry was a theory *within* alchemy. Like Geber, the great early chemists were also alchemists. Sir Isaac Newton was an alchemist, as was Robert Boyle, whose book *The Sceptical Chymist,* published in 1661, is considered the first book on modern chemistry.

Beginning in the nineteenth century with the Age of Reason, interest in alchemy waned and was superseded by more rational sciences. At this point, alchemy underwent its own transformation. Psychologist Carl Jung and esotericist Mary Anne Atwood, among others, said that alchemy's goal had never been to transform physical lead into physical gold. Rather, it was the transmutation of the soul of the alchemist. Psychological and spiritual alchemists contended that "lead" was base, unevolved human nature, while "gold" was the elevated soul, close to God.

The oldest extant book about alchemy, *Cheirokmeta* by Zosimos of Panopolis (circa 300 CE), states that alchemy was a gateway to spiritual salvation and the work was of psychic transformation. The same is true in Chinese alchemy, which distinguished between *waidan* (external alchemy) and *neidan* (internal alchemy). Yet alchemists like Zosimos always worked in labs, distilling, purifying, and extracting substances. Contrary to the assertions of Jung and others, their work was not metaphorical; it operated on both the physical and spiritual levels.

Today, both occultists and scientists have re-created and validated physical experiments of ancient alchemists. Using modern lab equipment, they've discovered that the obscure codes and notations in medieval alchemical notebooks weren't necessarily metaphors. For example, an experiment described as the "net of Athena" produces a chemical compound resembling a net, and colorfully named creatures (such as the "green lion") might refer to the color of a chemical in an experiment (such as green vitriol).

Psychological and spiritual alchemy are important movements within occultism. Alchemy is currently practiced by occultists and healers with a wide range of motives, from plant purity and communion with the planets to elixirs of life extension and healing the soul—and more. Still misunderstood, alchemy is nonetheless alive and well. Let's look further into this occult practice.

✦→⊢ MEET ⊢←✦ PARACELSUS

Paracelsus (1493/94–1541), born Theophrastus von Hohenheim in Switzerland, was a physician, chemist, Hermetic philosopher, theologian, and alchemist. The (probably illegitimate) son of a physician and a bondswoman, he struggled all his life with the low status of his birth, despite his accomplishments. Called the "father of toxicology," he introduced the idea of targeting disease with drugs, rather than "balancing humors," and insisted that physicians needed knowledge of chemistry. He defined the correspondence between disease, medicine, and plants.

Paracelsus was revered in Rosicrucianism (an occult movement that arose in the early seventeenth century), especially in Germany. Indeed, some Paracelsians believe that he found the elixir of immortality and that his grave is empty.

UNDERSTANDING ALCHEMY

The ultimate goal of alchemy is to fully understand and transform nature. Its four goals (the alkahest, the panacea, transmutation, and the homunculus) all reflect this: to understand and perfect the microcosm is to become closer to the macrocosm. This is similar to the Kabbalistic concept of healing the wounds of the world—unsurprisingly, many early Kabbalists were alchemists (see page 111).

Nature, the alchemist believes, has broken since the "fall" of Adam and Eve. By transforming and elevating individual metals (microcosm), the Earth itself could be healed and come closer to God (macrocosm).

To appreciate alchemists as scientists, it's crucial to understand that science was not considered separate from spirituality until the Enlightenment in the seventeenth and eighteenth centuries—medicine was not so very different from theology, and the laboratory contained the mind and soul as well as chemicals, plants, and metals. This can all get a little confusing; alchemy was purposely obscure and metaphorical, and it straddles mysticism and science in a way unfamiliar to most people today. The components of alchemy, though, can be understood as metals, planets, elements, and principles, as we'll see.

METALS AND PLANETS

Alchemists understood astrology. Fortunately, you've read a bit about it, because the planets and elements are again important (see the chart on page 49). Let's look at how the seven primary metals of the alchemist correspond to the planets:

METAL	PLANET	SIGN	ELEMENT
Gold	Sun	Leo	Fire
Silver	Moon	Cancer	Water
Quicksilver (mercury)	Mercury	Gemini and Virgo	Aether (combining Water, Earth, and Air)
Copper	Venus	Taurus and Libra	Water
Iron	Mars	Aries and Scorpio	Fire
Tin	Jupiter	Sagittarius and Pisces	Water
Lead	Saturn	Capricorn and Aquarius	Earth

Lead is the "lowest" metal, the furthest from God, and gold is the highest. The metals are seen as a progression, and each planetary spirit is contained in its corresponding metal.

You may notice that the element corresponding to the planet/metal isn't always the same as the element of the astrological sign of that planet/metal. Look at how that adds insight into each sign. For instance, notice how Earthy Taurus and Airy Libra are each touched by Venus's Water. Taurus tends to the sensual, and Libra to the romantic—both Venusian.

MERCURY AND SULFUR AND SALT

Zosimos (see page 84) was among the first alchemists to define the sulfur-mercury theory. Sulfur was "pneuma," a volatile spirit, and mercury was "soma," a nonvolatile body. But chemists know that mixing mercury and sulfur creates mercuric sulfide, or cinnabar—a toxic compound. Alchemists used code names (*decknamen*) for their work: sulfur wasn't sulfur; mercury wasn't mercury. Thus, the perfect mix they describe is elusive.

The "marriage" of mercury and sulfur also represents male and female, positive and negative, earth and spirit. Alchemical art is full of these two spirits, symbolized by a naked man and woman, merging sexually and becoming a hermaphrodite—often a two-headed being of a perfected two-gender body. (Note: The word "hermaphrodite" is used in alchemical texts, and thus it is used in this book, even though today we'd use the term "intersex." Alchemy can be seen as heteronormative but also transcends gender.)

When Paracelsus introduced the three primes (*tria prima*), the dynamic was no longer a simple male-female polarity, but body (salt), spirit/higher mind (mercury), and soul/emotion/desire (sulfur). I like to think of it as corresponding to astrology's fixed (salt), mutable (mercury), and cardinal (sulfur). Paracelsus believed the building blocks of the universe were the four elements *plus* the three primes. The universe is still polar in the tria prima theory, but salt/body unites and mediates between mercury/female/spirit and sulfur/male/soul. Today, some alchemists are Paracelsian, while some adhere to the sulfur-mercury theory.

THE FOUR ELEMENTS REVISITED

The four elements were long established in Greek philosophy, but they were added to alchemy by Geber. Fire and Air are upward-seeking, rising to the heavens, with Fire being the most volatile. Earth and Water are downward-seeking, flowing from above, with Earth being the most stable.

Combining elements can nullify them, but it can also create a unified whole that leads to transcendence of polarity—in alchemy, this is called the *coniunctio oppositorum* (the conjunction of opposites). The balance of the four elements and transcendence of polarity are goals in both psychological and physical alchemy.

The Alchemical Scientist
and Laboratory

Old illustrations of alchemy labs look both mysterious and familiar. Alchemical laboratories were stocked with equipment used by chemists today—some equipment has not even needed to be modernized. Alchemists performed their operations (see page 94) both physically and psychically. Thus, a lab might have had a Bible, an altar for prayer, and illustrations used as meditative mandalas, as well as a furnace, distillation equipment, crucibles, funnels, baths, flasks, retorts, and so on. This equipment has become associated with sorcery and evil in the popular imagination (think of the Evil Queen's laboratory in *Snow White and the Seven Dwarfs*).

◇→ MEET ←◇
MIRIAM THE JEWESS

The first alchemist and chemist known to history was Miriam the Jewess (aka Mary/Maria the Jewess/Maria the Prophetess), who lived in Alexandria sometime between the first and third century CE. She left no writings but is quoted extensively by Zosimos—and continued to be quoted for the next 1,700 years.

Miriam invented significant laboratory equipment, including glass equipment, which was not easy in those days. The bain-marie, a double boiler, bears her name. Her inventions include the *tribikos* (a three-armed alembic) and the *kerotakis*, both important variations on distilling equipment. She is one of the few alchemists said to have found the Philosopher's Stone.

Today, we distill alcohol and also use the word "distill" metaphorically—to boil something down to its essence. The process involves heating a liquid until it becomes a gas and then cooling it so that what remains is the purest (distilled) form. Distilling equipment uses a condenser, an alembic, or a retort to capture the cooled liquid. Since different liquids vaporize and reliquefy at different temperatures, a distiller might have multiple condensers. (Dry distilling heats a solid until it becomes gas.) The furnace and crucible are used for heating, and baths are used to expose substances to liquids to transform them.

TYPES OF ALCHEMY

Alchemy started in Alexandria, in Hellenized Egypt, somewhere between 300 BCE and the first century CE. By around 400 CE, it entered an important Islamic period, and from there reached medieval Europe in 1144, in the form of the *Book of the Composition of Alchemy,* translated from Arabic into Latin that year. This entire thousand-year history tells a single story: the story of Western alchemy. Alchemy from India appears to be similar to Western alchemy, but scholarship on the subject leaves many unknowns, whereas Chinese alchemy, different from Western, is well understood.

In many ways, the more important variations of alchemy are *what* is being transformed. Metals? Plants? The human soul? Let's explore.

WESTERN ALCHEMY

In looking at the history of alchemy so far, we've met luminaries of the field, like Miriam and Zosimos. Their work, primarily in Alexandria, defined alchemy and its goals. They built laboratories, invented equipment, and explored the spiritual meaning of their physical experiments.

Most of the development of alchemy in the medieval period happened in the Islamic world, as exemplified by Geber. It was not until the Renaissance and Paracelsus that a new form of alchemy emerged. Agrippa and Paracelsus were both students of the German Hermeticist Johannes Trithemius, but their approaches were different. Agrippa's innovation was blending alchemy and astrology with Christian Kabbalah (see page 112). Paracelsus, meanwhile, focused more on medicine and on his new theory of tria prima (see page 88). The Hermetic alchemy they practiced had its peak in the Renaissance, guided by the *Emerald Tablet* of Hermes Trismegistus.

So when discussing "Western" or "Hermetic" alchemy, we're talking about the scientific and spiritual practice of seeking transformation simultaneously within the laboratory and within the self by merging polarities into a mystical hermaphrodite (that also creates/extends life, creates gold, etc.).

◇→⊣ MEET ⊢←◇
NICHOLAS FLAMEL

Nicholas Flamel (1330–1418) may be best known as the alchemist from *Harry Potter and the Sorcerer's Stone*, but he was a real person. A scribe and bookseller, the legend of his alchemical knowledge began 200 years after his death, when *Exposition of the Hieroglyphical Figures* was published, with Flamel supposedly the author.

"Flamel" reports purchasing *The Book of the Sacred Magic of Abramelin the Mage* from a Jew fleeing persecution. From it, he learned alchemy, eventually finding the Philosopher's Stone. Was it making gold that allowed a humble scribe to become so wealthy and generous? In fact, his wife brought a significant inheritance into their marriage. There's no contemporaneous evidence that Flamel was an alchemist.

Plant Alchemy

Practical alchemy applied to plants is called "spagyrics"—the process of breaking a plant down into its component parts and putting those parts back together in a purified form for the purpose of healing. Spagyrics (from the Greek *spao*, collect, and *ageiro*, extract) was invented by Paracelsus. It is based on extracting the three primes of a plant:

- ◆ **THE SOUL (SULFUR)** is the scent or the essential oils of a plant.
- ◆ **THE MIND (MERCURY)** is the tincture or the alcohol extract of the plant.
- ◆ **THE BODY (SALT)** is the crystallized substance contained in the ash of the burned plant, or its salt.

Spagyrics is a spiritual as well as physical process. All work should be started in the planetary hour corresponding to the specific plant and work (see page 158).

Psychological and Spiritual Alchemy

Spiritual alchemy is the redemption of the self through alchemy. The seven operations of alchemy—the *Magnum Opus* (see page 94)—are seen as a process of inner transformation, unrelated to the physical. In fact, Carl Jung believed that alchemists only *thought* their experiments were chemical. In the Age of Reason, Jung and other spiritual alchemists reshaped the very nature of alchemy, removing it from the laboratory entirely.

Chinese Alchemy

No one is sure how old Chinese alchemy is, but by 165 BCE, there were edicts against some of its practices. Chinese alchemy is rooted in Taoism, the philosophy of harmony and balance. Naturally, it uses the five Chinese elements: Metal, Water, Wood, Fire, and Earth.

STOCKING YOUR SPAGYRICS LABORATORY

Spagyrics is far more accessible to the beginner than working with metals. Naturally, you'll need **REFERENCE MATERIALS** for herbs, planets, and detailed spagyric instructions.

To make tinctures, you'll want a collection of **MASON JARS** with glass tops, or parchment paper for ones with metal tops. For the finished tincture, you'll need small, dark-colored **BOTTLES WITH DROPPER TOPS**.

You'll also need grain **ALCOHOL**, vodka, or grappa (grape alcohol), **STRING** or **TWINE**, and a **MORTAR AND PESTLE**. **FUNNELS**, **FILTERS**, and **CHEESECLOTH** are needed for straining and decanting. If you're making numerous tinctures, you'll need labels for your jars. (Tinctures can also be made with a **PERCOLATION CONE** in about 48 hours, saving weeks of time.)

Calcination (see page 94) is a very smoky procedure. In addition to a **CERAMIC BOILER**, you'll want an outdoor **CAMP STOVE**. You'll need **SPOONS**, **BOWLS**, **GLASS CONTAINERS** for pouring water, and heavy-duty **OVEN MITTS**.

To extract the essential oil, you'll need some form of **DISTILLING EQUIPMENT**: a retort or alembic, as well as more droppers and jars.

Finally, remember that spagyrics is a spiritual process as well as a physical one. Alchemy is a tradition replete with complex and beautiful **ART**. You can find amazing woodcuts of the Rebis (the divine hermaphrodite), for example. Hanging such art in your workspace for meditation is an ancient tradition.

The primary goal of Chinese alchemy was originally to create an elixir of immortality. The makeup of "alchemical gold" was a central mystery. Early experimenters thought a "fake gold" that contained mercury—cinnabar—was key. Unfortunately, ingesting mercury is poisonous, so alchemists switched to real gold as an ingredient. Today, "inner alchemy" in China seeks to balance the life force and the inner female and male elements.

MAGNUM OPUS—THE GREAT WORK (IN THE LAB AND THE SELF)

At its heart, alchemy takes something apart (the world, the self, a metal, or a plant) and puts it back together in a holier and more perfect form. This is called *solve et coagula*: dissolve and conjoin. Through a series of stages, that something is destroyed; separated into its component parts, each of which is perfected; and then reintegrated. The parts are elements or polarities (at least metaphorically gendered), but through the alchemical process, separation is shown to be an illusion: genders are really the divine hermaphrodite, the snake swallows its own tail, and transcendence is achieved.

Alchemy uses seven operations for this transformation. These operations—calcination, dissolution, separation, conjunction, fermentation, distillation, and coagulation—are commonly condensed into three stages: Black (calcination and dissolution), White (separation and conjunction), and Red (fermentation, distillation, and coagulation). Together, they comprise the *Magnum Opus*—the Great Work. (Some alchemists include Yellow between White and Red, isolating fermentation.)

These operations are not done in linear order and are often repeated. Let's look at what's involved.

NIGREDO: BLACKENING

The Black stage begins with the application of Fire and Water. First is calcination, turning something to ashes or otherwise transforming it through fire. Second is dissolution, in which the substance is dissolved in water. In alchemy, the color black represents death and decay.

♦ **IN THE LABORATORY:** A substance is heated until it is turned to ash, or the exterior, impure parts (the "dross") are turned to ash (leaving an unburned core), or it is bathed in an acidic "liquid fire," such as sulfuric acid. The ashes are then dissolved in water or another liquid solution.

♦ IN A PLANT: First, a tincture is made (see page 97). This mercury/spirit is set aside. The remaining plant substance is cooked until ashen (calcinated). Water is added and cooked off repeatedly (dissolution) to create a salt/body.

♦ IN THE SELF: We "go through the fire" when we face our ego and release vanity. Sometimes we experience trauma that changes us in this way. We "dissolve" into the truth of meditation or self-examination, swimming the waters of the unconscious mind.

ALBEDO: WHITENING

Having applied Fire and Water, next up is Air (separation) and Earth (conjunction). Here the substance produced by the Black phase is separated and made pure, symbolically applying Air. Then, in conjunction, the symbolic "sacred marriage" of opposites occurs. That which is separated is found, spiritually, to be truly one, and is combined. Because conjunction is Earth, it *grounds* the results of the operation. White represents purification in alchemy.

♦ IN THE LABORATORY: The product of dissolution is filtered in some way, possibly using a fractional distillation process. The separated results are saved, and then, in conjunction, brought back together. A catalyst or acid might be used to force this joining of separated components.

♦ IN A PLANT: The salt is further purified and separated from insoluble matter (separation and dissolution).

♦ IN THE SELF: Separation involves examining the self and looking at each piece dispassionately. *Is this part of me that I instinctively pull away from actually an inner healer?* This is "shadow work"—facing the parts of ourselves we are loathe to face. Conjunction is reintegration: we bring the shadow to the light and marry the two.

RUBEDO: REDDENING

The Red phase is almost a return to the earlier operations. Fermentation is a kind of death and resurrection, bringing new life from dead matter. The fermented product is then distilled. Finally, coagulation brings everything together, producing gold or the Philosopher's Stone. Red symbolizes intense heat and spiritual fire.

♦ **IN THE LABORATORY:** First, the material must be rotted. As fermentation begins, a waxy yellow substance emerges. The fermented product is then distilled, often many times, seeking a purer and purer substance. The distillate is then sublimated or precipitated. In chemistry, creating a gas from a solid without an intermediate liquid is called "sublimation," while creating a solid from a solution is called "precipitation." In coagulation, the fermented distillate is merged with the remains of fermentation. This solid is the final product of alchemy.

♦ **IN A PLANT:** For a spagyric tincture, the tincture is mixed with the salt. For a spagyric elixir, the tincture is fermented and distilled. Distillation allows the oil (sulfur/soul) to be drawn off and separated. The tincture, oil, and salt are then combined into an elixir (coagulation).

♦ **IN THE SELF:** In fermentation, we actually live as the new, conjoined self we've created; we take our healing out for a spin. This allows us to see what needs to be distilled—that is, what further inner work needs to be done. We refine and perfect the inner work. Coagulation is a perfected self: a true integration of body, mind, and spirit. Most of us cycle through, starting over, getting closer and closer, without ever achieving this exalted state.

MAKING A TINCTURE

Making a tincture is the simplest work of practical alchemy. It requires no special equipment and can give you a sense of the work of the alchemist, in addition to a useful concoction. Begin by choosing a plant based on its occult properties (see page 158) to give your tincture a purpose. If you wish to avoid alcohol, you can make a glycerite instead of a tincture by replacing the alcohol with glycerin. Use three parts food-grade glycerin to one part distilled water for dried plants. (I am not sure how a glycerite would interact with the salt or essential oil in spagyrics.)

YOU'LL NEED:

About 2 cups of a fresh (or a half cup dried) plant of your choosing

A few inches of string (if using a fresh plant)

A mortar and pestle

Two jars with tight lids, one big enough for your herbs and the other for the tincture

Grain alcohol or vodka (enough to fill the herb jar)

Parchment paper (if using jars with metal tops)

Cloth

A strainer or filter

INSTRUCTIONS:

1. Find the planet corresponding to your plant and its planetary hours (see page 158). Begin preparations during the planetary hour of your work.

2. If using a fresh plant, wrap the stem in string and hang it by the tail of the string until it is dried out. If using a dried plant, you can skip straight to the next step. Begin the next step on the planetary hour.

3. Once the plant is dry, say a prayer or meditate on the purpose of your tincture.

CONTINUED ▶

4. Tear the dried plant into small pieces with your hands if necessary. (Do not use a knife; the alchemical properties of metals overpower the delicate alchemy of plants.)
5. Grind the dried plant with the mortar and pestle.
6. Place the ground dried plant in the herb jar, filling no more than ¾ of the jar, and then fill completely with the alcohol and seal. (If the jar has a metal lid, place parchment paper over the mouth of the jar before sealing, so that the contents of the jar aren't exposed to any metal.)
7. Wrap the jar in cloth and put it in a dark place.
8. Shake your mixture every one to three days. (If the lid of your jar is metal, be careful not to let the liquid touch the lid.)
9. In three to six weeks, pour the liquid through the filter into the smaller jar and use your tincture for the purpose you created it in the dosage recommended from your source.

ALCHEMICAL UNDERPINNINGS OF THE OCCULT

Our journey through alchemy took us through science and history and into laboratories. Although challenging to understand, alchemy hides underneath much of modern occultism.

♦ The *Hermetica* called alchemy one of the "three pillars" of knowledge.

♦ The mystical relationship between the macrocosm and the microcosm ("As above, so below") is fundamental to understanding alchemy as a spiritual practice.

♦ As Miriam the Jewess said, "One must join the male and the female and then you will find what is sought." This is a core occult principle, even to those who've never read a word about alchemy. (It can also be a transcendent and healing principle for queer and trans occultists who get pretty tired of the separation of male and female throughout occultism.)

These alchemical ideas are everywhere in the occult. The separation and transcendence of polarity is work that occurs both outside and within. Astrology and alchemy together reshape our understanding of the cosmos and the Earth, as well as of numbers and colors. The simplest Wiccan ritual or the most chaotic of chaos magic bears the marks of these ideas.

CHAPTER 6

KABBALAH

The study of Kabbalah is fundamental to many occult philosophies. However, its origin is not in the occult but in Judaism.

Kabbalah was originally, and remains, Jewish mysticism. It begins in the oldest Jewish mystical text, the *Sefer Yetzirah*, which may date back as far as 200 BCE (scholars are still figuring it out). The most important text on the Kabbalah (still studied by scholars and mystics) is the thirteenth-century work *The Zohar*, which arose during a flowering of Jewish intellectualism in Spain. This dense and complex text remains the most important work on Kabbalah. It was written by Moses de León, who claimed he "discovered" it and that it dated from the second century.

In the thirteenth century, Christian mystic Ramon Llull saw Kabbalah as a potent tool for converting Jews to Christianity, but the idea of a Christian Kabbalah didn't take off until the early Renaissance. It's important to understand that the late Middle Ages and early Renaissance was a period of intense antisemitism. In Spain, Jews were forcibly converted to Catholicism or driven out of the country by the hundreds of thousands. The beauty and mysticism of the Kabbalah was embraced by Christians eager to remove it from its Jewish roots. Part of the purpose of Christian Kabbalah remained conversion.

"Hermetic Kabbalah" refers to the Western occult study of the subject. It, too, is a product of the fifteenth century. Agrippa's *Three Books of Occult Philosophy* was seminal in combining Kabbalah with occult disciplines such as astrology, ritual magic, and numerology.

In chapter 7, we'll talk about the importance of the Hermetic Order of the Golden Dawn ("Golden Dawn" for short). It is through this magical order that Kabbalah fully entered "occult mainstream" (to use an oxymoron), tying the Kabbalistic Tree of Life to its core ritual practices, its magical tools, and the tarot, among other occult practices. Kabbalah is fundamental to understanding Hermeticism as passed to us today through this influential magical order and its many offshoots.

However, there are people who feel that Kabbalah shouldn't be a part of Western magic at all, since it amounts to cultural appropriation of a Jewish tradition by non-Jews. They point out that Christian and Hermetic Kabbalah were originally purposely antisemitic, and even today, some Hermeticists claim that Kabbalah originated in classical Greece and was later adopted by Jews. This is completely false and exists only to erase Judaism's enormous contribution to mystical thought.

I am Jewish. I respect Jewish occultists who have this point of view. But Kabbalah is so deeply embedded in almost every part of Western occultism that removing it would be like removing the hydrogen from water; it cannot be done.

Instead, I'd suggest that any non-Jew studying Kabbalah make sure to be respectful of Jewish culture (including making an effort to correctly pronounce Hebrew). Listen to Jewish voices and take antisemitism seriously, doing your part to combat it. If you're lecturing Jews on their own tradition, you're doing it wrong.

You might ask, "What is the purpose of studying Kabbalah?" I'd argue you can't study Western occultism in an informed way if you don't understand the part of Kabbalah known as the Tree of Life (at least a little), due to its ubiquity. More specifically, here's why you'd study the Tree:

♦ As a tool of understanding the universe and creation, from the vastness of ineffable infinity to the concrete and natural world we live in.

- As a tool of understanding the self, flowing in the opposite direction, from the physical body to the transcendent ("As above, so below").
- As a tool of understanding the interplay of energies present in a wide array of ritual experiences, in order to deepen those experiences.
- As a way to understand the energetic interplay in day-to-day life and thus gain greater power and integration in life.
- As a vast system of correspondences that allow you to add power to virtually any ritual or act of magic.

With these purposes in mind, let's learn more.

UNDERSTANDING KABBALAH

The core of understanding Hermetic Kabbalah is the Tree of Life and its component parts. This is a vast field of study, as Kabbalah is a system of magic, meditation, self-actualization, and prayer, depending upon how it's approached. But learning the basics is fairly straightforward.

THE TREE OF LIFE

The glyph known as the Tree of Life (see page 100) is a map of creation first introduced in *The Zohar*. It arises from a simple yet profound question: If God is infinite, vast, and perfect, why should God bother to create a universe, rather than simply *be* perfect? From here comes the idea that creation emerges gradually, bit by bit, as God moves from the infinite toward something finite and real. Creation is viewed as a kind of back-and-forth energetic flow, until finally arriving at the world—and us.

The infinite, unknowable, eternal perfection of God is not a part of the Tree; it is outside and beyond the Tree and is known as *Ain Soph* (endless). Each step in the flow of creation—from the most cosmic to the most worldly—is seen as a sphere (in Hebrew, *sephi-rah*). Each sephirah is a container of a particular kind of energy. The *sephirot* (plural of sephirah) are aspects of God, reality, and the self.

THE 10 SEPHIROT

At the top of the tree is **KETER** (Crown). Keter is the universe prior to the big bang; it is undifferentiated everythingness. The only difference between Ain Soph and Keter is that Ain Soph is too vast even to be described, but Keter has a potential to create, and so it can be placed upon the tree.

Next comes **CHOKMAH** (Wisdom). (Note that "ch" in Hebrew is pronounced in the back of the throat, like the German "ach" or the Scottish "loch." Hebrew does not have a sound like the "ch" in "cheese.") Chokmah is force, energy, and ceaseless motion, and is often seen as male—the supernal Father.

Third is **BINAH** (Understanding). Binah is form, shape, and limitation—the supernal Mother. Binah is a container that holds Chokmah. If undifferentiated force is chaos, undifferentiated form is stasis, but together, they are possibility and move us toward manifestation.

CHESED (Compassion or Lovingkindness) is an infinite outpouring of love. Imagine force and form coming together and moving in the direction of creation. Why? Love—love overflow-ing, uncontainable, and vast. We've moved toward manifestation, but without Chesed—without infinite, compassionate love for manifestation—creation won't proceed.

GEVURAH (Strength) judges, imposes law, and determines limits. Gevurah and Chesed interact like "good cop" and "bad cop"—one wants only to be kind, and the other wants only to follow the rules. Too much Chesed is indulgent; too much Gevurah is tyrannical.

TIPHERET (Beauty) is the very center of the Tree. It is halfway between Keter and Malkut and is touched by every other sephirah.

Tipheret mediates between Chesed and Gevurah, and in a way, between Chokmah and Binah as well. Tipheret is death and rebirth, the glorious coming together of opposites, and perfect harmony achieved by balancing extremes.

NETZACH (Victory) is kindness and endurance. Netzach urges toward connection, passion, and giving, but like Chokmah (they are vertically aligned), Netzach's energies are without form.

HOD (Splendor) gives form to Netzach, receiving Netzach's desire and connection and shaping it. Hod is doing, communicating, and self-actualizing. Hod is ego, rationality, and learning.

YESOD (Foundation) mediates between Netzach and Hod, and also between Tipheret above and the world (Malkut) below. Yesod is dreams, the unconscious, and ritual trance.

MALKUT (Kingdom) is the world but not quite the world. The Tree brings us to creation, but Malkut is creation with the presence of the Godhead. Ordinary life is not exactly Malkut. But if you're having an ordinary day and stop to have a conversation about something spiritual, the spark generated by that conversation is Malkut. Malkut's other name is SHEKINAH, the goddess of the Tree, and She is present whenever ordinary Earth is elevated just a tiny bit.

The top-down journey through the sephirot just described is known as the "lightning flash" and is a traditional path from God to humans. Another journey is up, from microcosm to macrocosm. In that direction, you begin in reality, with a desire to expand consciousness (Malkut), which you achieve through meditation, trance, and work with your unconscious mind (Yesod). This leads to an enhanced understanding of yourself (Hod) and a deeper sense of connection to others (Netzach). Here, you begin to see the possibility of true "cosmic consciousness," you begin to sense the interconnectedness of all things, and you experience a sense of grace (Tipheret). From this point of view, you become aware of the injustice of the world (Gevurah) and are flooded with lovingkindness toward all (Chesed).

Most occultists say that Chesed is the highest a human can experience while in the mortal body. The sephirot atop the Tree are truly transcendent and beyond mortal reach. We can only reach toward them and contemplate them: First, the loving and terrifying concept of the very shape of the universe, the infinite womb; fate itself, containment. Then, the overwhelming concept of the force of the universe, the infinite expansion of energy. Finally, the Oneness from which they emerge.

Let's look more deeply at the Tree of Life.

THE TRIADS

Looking at the glyph of the Tree (see page 100), we can see it's made up of three distinct triangles with Malkut hanging out on its own at the bottom. Each triangle forms a kind of dialectic between force and form, or between expansion and contraction, with synthesis and balance at the center. Often, the left and right are gendered.

- ♦ **THE SUPERNAL TRIAD** of Keter-Chokmah-Binah is force and form in its purest and most cosmic aspect, with their synthesis being the very source of creation. Chokmah and Binah are called Father and Mother, but we're meant to understand them as fundamentally One.
- ♦ **THE ETHICAL TRIAD** of Chesed-Gevurah-Tipheret gives shape to the supernal through the force of love and the form of law. Gevurah structures and restricts, while Chesed expands and frees, but the truth lies in mediating between them (Tipheret).
- ♦ **THE MAGICAL OR ASTRAL TRIAD** of Netzach-Hod-Yesod is the closest to human consciousness and expresses the beginnings of interaction and individuation. The force of desire and the form of self are mediated in the unconscious mind. These are the most human of the sephirot, taking us to Malkut.

DA'AT

Looking again at the picture of the Tree, you'll see there's kind of a hole between the Supernal and Ethical triads. There's an "invisible" sephirah, left off most pictures of the Tree, called *Da'at* (Knowledge). Da'at is perfected knowledge, such that all sephirot are united, and it is applied knowledge, where wisdom and understanding are made manifest.

It is left off the Tree for several reasons: First, because the *Sefer Yetzirah* says that there should be exactly 10, not 11, spheres. Second, because it represents the fruit plucked by Eve in the Garden of Eden and so is no longer on the Tree. Third, because Da'at would complete the Tree, and we are not perfected. The Tree with Da'at would be a perfected universe—not ours, which has evil in it.

As I mentioned, human consciousness can't ascend above the fourth sephirah. The void space below the Supernal Triad is called the "Abyss," which can't be traversed. It's a kind of glitch in reality. Human beings act against our own self-interest. We know what to do (Binah, understanding) but don't do it. Da'at (applied knowledge) is acting upon what we know. Refusing to do so is the human condition. Da'at is invisible because there *is* an Abyss.

THE PILLARS

The Tree has three vertical columns: the Pillars of Severity, Mercy, and Mildness. Severity is on the left, containing Binah, Gevurah, and Hod. It is the path of form: it contains and limits, and is often called female. Mercy is on the right, containing Chokmah, Chesed, and Netzach. It is the path of force, it expands and activates, and it is called male. In the center is the Pillar of Mildness, containing Keter, Tipheret, Yesod, and Malkut, as well as Da'at. This is the path of balance. It overcomes dualism and mediates difference.

The Four Worlds

Each sephirah emanates on four levels in four worlds. *Atzilut*, the world of Fire, is considered the most direct access to God. *Briyah* corresponds to Water, emotion, experience, and intuition in Hermetic Kabbalah, but Air, mind, and pure thought in Jewish Kabbalah. *Yetzirah* is Hermetic Air/Jewish Water. *Assiyah* is the world of Earth. It is the physical plane of creation.

The Paths

The Tree shows 22 paths between the sephirot. This adds further nuance to our understanding of the Tree; there's not just Binah or Gevurah, for instance, but the path between them, a place where their energies meet and blend. Each path corresponds to one of the 22 letters of the Hebrew alphabet.

Correspondences

Because Kabbalah describes all of reality, correspondences are nearly infinite. As we saw in previous chapters, correspondences are a powerful aid to ritual, magic, and understanding. Hermetics in particular innovated a syncretic, cross-cultural set of Kabbalistic correspondences, as we can see in the following chart.

SEPHIRAH	PLANET	COLOR	NUMBER	ARCHANGEL
Keter	The "cosmic swirl"	White	1	Metatron
Chokmah	The zodiac	Gray	2	Ratziel
Binah	Saturn	Black	3	Tzaphkiel
Chesed	Jupiter	Blue	4	Tzadkiel
Gevurah	Mars	Red	5	Kamael
Tipheret	Sun	Yellow	6	Raphael
Netzach	Venus	Green	7	Haniel
Hod	Mercury	Orange	8	Michael
Yesod	Moon	Purple	9	Gabriel
Malkut	Earth	Citrine, olive, russet, and black (seen as a quartered circle)	10	Sandalphon

PLACING THE TREE ON YOUR BODY

This is a meditation I do often, and it becomes quite easy in time. The universe and its cosmic energies are part of you. Making a conscious connection between the two can be transformative. Performing this meditation regularly will allow you eventually to feel connections you weren't previously aware of.

Note: The Tree on your body is seen from the outside, so Chokmah, Chesed, and Netzach are on the left side of your body (see page 100).

INSTRUCTIONS:

1. Breathe deeply and center yourself.
2. Visualize a white sphere floating just at the crown of your head. Say, "Keter. Crown."
3. Visualize a gray sphere at the left side of your face. Say, "Chokmah. Wisdom."
4. Visualize a black sphere at the right side of your face. Say, "Binah. Understanding."
5. Visualize your left arm as royal blue. Say, "Chesed. Compassion."
6. Visualize your right arm as red. Say, "Gevurah. Strength."
7. Visualize your solar plexus as bright yellow. Say, "Tipheret. Beauty."
8. Visualize your left leg as emerald green. Say, "Netzach. Victory."
9. Visualize your right leg as orange. Say, "Hod. Splendor."
10. Visualize your genitalia as deep purple. Say, "Yesod. Foundation."
11. Visualize yourself standing on a quartered circle, with one quarter each citrine, russet, olive, and black. Say, "Malkut. Kingdom."
12. Now reverse the steps, visualizing and saying Malkut, Yesod, Hod, Netzach, Tipheret, Gevurah, Chesed, Binah, Chokmah, and Keter.
13. End by contemplating the infinity beyond.

FORMS OF KABBALAH

As we've learned, the Jewish roots of Kabbalah go back to antiquity. The Tree of Life was first seen in *The Zohar* in the thirteenth century. This form of mysticism ultimately had Christian and Hermetic offshoots. I've touched upon this, but let's explore further.

JEWISH KABBALAH

The word "Kabbalah" means tradition, or to receive. It is the study of the transcendent and mystical meaning of the Hebrew numbers and letters as the building blocks of creation. We touched on gematria in chapter 4; the reason gematria is thought to work is because the letters themselves come from God, and thus the words and numbers they form can be a gateway to God.

Jews were driven from Spain by the Alhambra Decree in 1492; five years later, they were expelled from Portugal as well. Exiled Iberian mystics settled in present-day Israel, in the town of Safed. It was here, a few years later, that Isaac Luria reinterpreted *The Zohar* as a guide to a life of holiness that can help heal the world. Lurianic Kabbalah is influential in Judaism even today.

Many early Kabbalists were alchemists. The idea of mystically healing the world is shared by both; alchemists heal the world through transmutation, and Kabbalists through the performance of *mitzvot*, the fulfillment of commandments. Early Kabbalists even corresponded the metals to the sephirot.

Jewish Kabbalists are often opposed to the occult; magic and divination have long been forbidden in Judaism. "Practical Kabbalah," using Kabbalah for magic and divination, was once practiced, but it was forbidden by Isaac Luria and is not a normal part of Judaism today.

ISAAC LURIA

Isaac Luria (1534–1572), known as *Ha-Ari* (the Lion), was born in Jerusalem and raised in Egypt. At age 15, already a great scholar, he married his cousin. By age 22, he was living a deeply mystical life. He moved to Safed to study with Moses Cordovero, an authority on *The Zohar*.

Luria's writings were gathered after his death by Rabbi Chaim Vital, primarily in *Etz Chayim* (Tree of Life). His innovative ideas include healing the world (*tikkun olam*) through mitzvot, the idea that God contracted (*tzimtzum*) to create the world, and the idea that evil entered the world through a shattering (*shevirah*) of Divine Light. Luria died at age 38. His grave in Safed is considered a holy site.

CHRISTIAN KABBALAH

In Christian Kabbalah (sometimes spelled "Cabala"), Christ and Christianity are placed upon the Tree of Life, reinterpreting it as being about Jesus's life. Here, Keter is the Holy Spirit, Chokmah is the Father, Binah is Mary, and Tipheret is Jesus. Christian Kabbalah was absorbed into Hermetic Kabbalah during the Renaissance and doesn't exist as a distinct movement today, although some practitioners are interested in connecting Christ to the Tree of Life.

HERMETIC KABBALAH

As mentioned, Hermetic Kabbalah (sometimes spelled "Qabalah") refers to the Western occult study of the subject.

- ◆ It is a syncretic system. It takes Jewish Kabbalah and adds correspondences to Egyptian magic, Paganism, tarot, and virtually anything else that isn't nailed down.

- It has a greater emphasis on the Tree of Life. While Jewish Kabbalah certainly gives importance to the Tree, it also emphasizes gematria and other studies—the Tree is just a piece of it. In Hermetic Kabbalah, the Tree is pretty much the whole focus.
- Its purpose is both meditative and magical.

⟡ MEET ⟡
DION FORTUNE

Dion Fortune (1890–1946) was an occultist, author, magician, trance medium, and founder of the Fraternity of Inner Light. Born Violet Firth in North Wales, she used her family motto, *Deo, non Fortuna* (God, not luck), as a pen name.

Fortune began her spiritual training in Theosophy and reported trance contact with the "Ascended Masters" (formerly living spiritual beings), including "Master Jesus." In 1919, she joined Alpha et Omega, an offshoot of the Golden Dawn. Here she was trained extensively in ceremonial magic and Kabbalah, producing her greatest work, *The Mystical Qabalah*. Her many books remain deeply influential in occultism, Paganism, and Wicca.

USING THE KABBALAH

So far, our discussion of Kabbalah has focused quite a bit on mysticism and religion. You may be wondering how, exactly, it's the occult. It's definitely true that the primary "use" of Kabbalah is passive—meditation and contemplation. However, Kabbalah also makes an appearance in magic, as we'll see.

The Sephirot in Ritual and Magic

In chapters 3 and 4, we learned that the planets have meaningful energies. For example, to bring love into your life, the energies of Venus can be sought; to improve communication, connect to Mercury. Kabbalistic correspondences allow us to access planetary energies through the sephirot—Netzach for Venus and Hod for Mercury, in the examples on page 108.

The system of correspondences is vast. By deeply understanding a sephirah, you have its number, color, imagery, symbols, archangel, planet, and much more. If you meditate within that sphere, more of its wisdom might be revealed to you, and that, in turn, can deepen the magic and ritual you do that connects to it.

◇→┤ MEET ├←◇
ISRAEL REGARDIE

Israel Regardie (1907–1985) was an author, occultist, and ceremonial magician. He is most famous as the secretary of famed occultist Aleister Crowley and as the author of the definitive book *The Golden Dawn*. He also wrote two important books on Kabbalah.

Born in London to Orthodox Jewish parents, Regardie rejected traditional Judaism in his teens and spent his life exploring occultism and mysticism. He was interested in Theosophy, was a Rosicrucian initiate, and was also initiated into Stella Matutina, an offshoot of the Golden Dawn. Later in life, he became interested in psychology and became a chiropractor. He died in Sedona, Arizona.

Pathworking

Pathworking is a Kabbalistic meditative discipline where you mentally traverse the Tree of Life by "walking" one of the numbered paths in a specific direction, with instructions on what will be seen. For example, you might start in Malkut, clearly seeing its colors, one in each quarter of the round space you're in, and then leave that space and traverse the path to Yesod.

Pathworking in a group is read aloud from a script, while pathworking alone is generally achieved by recording the script and then playing it back while in a meditative state.

Pathworking is considered part of the "Great Work" of enlightenment in ceremonial magic and is a requirement for initiation into some magical systems.

Kabbalah in Magic: Numbers, Colors, and Symbols

The "Adding Numbers to Magic" exercise on page 116 explores different ways to add numbers to a spell—anything from the number of candles to the number of words spoken, limited only by your imagination. Kabbalah multiplies this many times. Again, using Netzach as an example, you have the number 7, the color green, the archangel Haniel, and the planet Venus, just to start.

I mentioned bringing love into your life by accessing the planetary energies of Venus. In Kabbalah, this corresponds to Netzach. A typical magical operation of Netzach might include making a green amulet with the planetary symbol and the name Haniel written in Hebrew. Names of God, Pagan gods, incenses, and more can be corresponded to the Tree, as can the tarot (see chapter 8). So for Netzach, you could burn rose incense during the operation while meditating on a 7 from the tarot (of whichever suit is appropriate for the operation).

ADDING NUMBERS TO MAGIC

In chapter 2, you learned to perform a magical cleansing of a tool. Choose another tool now to cleanse, and let's set up that spell again, this time with the power of numbers added to it.

First, determine the number you want to add to your spell. This will depend on the nature of the tool and the nature of the energy you want to bring. For example, if cleansing a pentacle (a traditional Wiccan tool of grounding and Earth), you might want to bring an earthy number to your spell; the Pythagorean chart on page 72 indicates that 4 is earthy. Here are a few ways to incorporate it:

→ You could perform the spell at 4 o'clock and/or on the fourth day of the month.

→ Set up the altar space where you'll do the spell with four candles or four crystals.

→ In chapter 2, the phrases in steps 1 through 4 each have three words.

→ Can you add a fourth word? How about, instead of "Air, bring wisdom," you say "Air, bring wisdom now"?

→ You're burning incense. Could you make an incense with exactly four ingredients?

Once you've figured out how to bring your desired number to this simple spell, follow the steps from the Magical Cleansing Spell (chapter 2, page 33).

KABBALAH THROUGHOUT MAGIC

We've seen that the Jewish mystical study known as Kabbalah dates to 200 BCE or earlier and began acquiring non-Jewish adherents thereafter. There are many connections to Kabbalah throughout the occult practices.

- ◆ The publication of *Three Books of Occult Philosophy* in 1531 cemented the place of Hermetic Kabbalah in occult thought. In the past 500 years, you'd be hard put to find a serious occultist who hasn't studied Kabbalah at least a little.

- ◆ Many magical lodges include Kabbalah in their studies (see chapter 7).

- ◆ Tarot has been explicitly tied to Kabbalah for more than a century.

- ◆ Occultists might invoke angels or write the Tetragrammaton (the four-letter Hebrew name of God) on magical talismans, and these derive from Kabbalah.

- ◆ Even the vernacular of the occult has been influenced by the Tree of Life. The "Left Hand Path" and "the Abyss" are ordinary parts of occult conversation even if people don't know they're talking about Kabbalah.

The Jewish mystics who first developed Kabbalah were not isolated from other mystical practices, and Kabbalah represents a magnificent cross-pollination of many components of occult philosophy. Although not an original part of Hermetic philosophy, it is a natural fit.

CEREMONIAL MAGIC

What is ceremonial magic? The well-known ceremonial magician (and my friend) Donald Michael Kraig (whom we'll meet later) disliked the term, saying magic was magic. Nonetheless, "ceremonial," "ritual," or "high" magic is usually distinguished from "natural" or "low" magic.

Ceremonial magic (CM) is a ritualized and structured method of performing magic primarily through the invocation of spiritual entities. The term was coined in a 1569 translation of a work by Heinrich Cornelius Agrippa, which said, "The partes of ceremoniall Magicke be Geocie, and Theurgie." That is, ceremonial magic consists of goetia and theurgy. "Goetia" is the invocation of demons and spirits, while "theurgy" is the invocation of God and higher angels.

If you have an image of CM in your head, it's probably something like a Renaissance-era, robed, bearded mage wielding a sword while standing in a circle of arcane symbols marked on the floor. That isn't far from the truth. CM, as we understand it today, did emerge in the Renaissance.

Magic becomes recognizably "ceremonial" with the beginning of the grimoire tradition. A grimoire is a magical textbook of spells, ceremonies, instructions, and miscellany. They began to appear in the Middle Ages. Famous ones from the twelfth through the fifteenth century include *The Sworn Book of Honorius*; *Picatrix*; *The Greater* and *Lesser Keys of Solomon the King*; and *The Book of the Sacred Magic of Abramelin the Mage*. They feature practices like drawing a circle on the ground and invoking demons, typical of what we'd call CM.

Grimoires continued to be written through the occult revival of the late nineteenth century, like Francis Barrett's *The Magus* in 1801. Despite being denounced as mere plagiarism of Agrippa's *Three Books of Occult Philosophy*, it became influential in occult circles and is considered a source document for the Golden Dawn (see page 101).

By the 1700s, Agrippa's influence meant that most CM was both Hermetic and Kabbalistic. Hermetics and Kabbalah, as well as alchemy, were all drawn on by the mystical order known as the Rosicrucians, a seventeenth-century secret society claiming access to ancient, esoteric wisdom. Although the Rosicrucian order has had ups and downs, it still exists in the form of the Ancient Mystical Order Rosae Crucis (AMORC).

The late eighteenth and nineteenth centuries introduced mystical religious philosophies that were studied by occultists, especially Theosophy (see page 121) and Swedenborgianism (based on the teachings of Emanuel Swedenborg). Most important, this period brought us Éliphas Lévi, perhaps the greatest magician of his time. Lévi was the first person to connect tarot to the Kabbalah. He worked extensively with grimoires and wrote important books on magic. Lévi was profoundly influential on the magicians who formed the Golden Dawn. His impact is still felt today.

The magicians of influential orders such as the Golden Dawn and its offshoots were nearly all Theosophists, Rosicrucians, Freemasons, or several of these and more, making the earlier groups important to our studies. They form the background from which more modern ceremonial magicians derive their practice.

From the seventeenth century to today, many (perhaps most) ceremonial magicians practice in "lodges" and similarly structured organizational groups. This underlines the influence of Freemasonry.

Where does Freemasonry come from? "Craft guilds"—trade organizations for crafts like stonemasonry, bookbinding, and baking—began in the twelfth century. Masons developed rituals, mystical lore, and secret oaths as the need for their more practical services declined. Modern Freemasonry retains the symbols of stonework in its rituals. What matters, though, is its influence on magicians—the structure of a Masonic lodge is not terribly different from that of a magical lodge, and degrees of initiation, oaths of secrecy, sacred tools, and secret passwords are shared features.

All this leads to the founding of the Golden Dawn in 1888. Its practice of CM combined the influences of everything we've read about so far, including astrology, alchemy, Hermetics, Kabbalah, grimoires, lodge structure, and more. Though it lasted only about a dozen years, the influence of the Golden Dawn is felt throughout the practice of magic today. Let's learn more.

◇→┤ MEET ├←◇
HELENA BLAVATSKY

Helena Petrovna Blavatsky (1831–1891), born Helena Petrovna Hahn in present-day Ukraine, was the cofounder of the Theosophical Society, the aim of which is to advance the ideas of Theosophy—a religion that combines Hinduism and Western mysticism. She is the author of *Isis Unveiled* and *The Secret Doctrine*. Born into the aristocracy, she studied spiritualism and claimed to be in touch with spiritual "Masters" in Tibet who trained her to be a psychic.

She was controversial throughout her life, with many of her claims deemed fraudulent, yet she amassed an enormous following. Blavatsky had a strong following in India and is responsible for coining the term "Lords of Karma" (criticized as a very Western interpretation of Hindu philosophy).

UNDERSTANDING CEREMONIAL MAGIC

Ceremonial magic works on certain principles, following certain rules, and existing within the framework of certain philosophies. We can approach this very broad and complex subject by starting with these principles.

"As Above, So Below"

We've repeated this concept many times in these pages; it's the core of Hermetics and the magic that flows from it. "As above, so below. As the universe, so the soul." We can create a microcosm of the universe within a magic circle, or within the meditative temple formed in our own minds. That above and below are mirrors of each other allows one small ritual to change the world.

Theurgy

As mentioned in chapter 1, for over a century, "high magic" has been concerned almost entirely with theurgy—communion with God or higher beings. In Thelema (see page 128), it's called "Knowledge and Conversation of the Holy Guardian Angel." While the grimoire tradition and much goetia is concerned with a host of results, such as finding treasure, gaining political power, and becoming invisible, from at least the time of the Golden Dawn, the purpose of most ceremonial magic is entirely psychospiritual.

Sources of Power

CM is understood to work because the magician accesses sources of power. Tools are made and magic is performed in the correct planetary hour (power from the planets), using the correct materials (power from the nature of those materials), and with the proper words being said (power from those words).

Ceremonial magicians, then, understand astrology and perhaps some alchemy—at least enough to know that metals and other materials have inherent power. They are learned enough to read grimoires, perhaps in multiple languages. Though a magician today might not understand Latin, Hebrew, and Greek, they will still pronounce these languages in invocations.

Notice the class barrier: proper materials might be expensive, and the correct time of day requires a certain amount of leisure, and then there's the acquisition of rare books. The Renaissance magician was not in remotely the same social class as a folk magician of the same period.

ANGELS, DEMONS, AND OTHER SPIRITS

CM might seem rooted in Judaism or Christianity because of Biblical references, but it is not religion. The entities invoked are not worshipped. Rather, they are used almost as tools, and this is true even when names of God are part of the ceremony.

Angels and demons predate the Bible and are found in ancient Near Eastern religions. Their mentions in the Bible and Quran are vastly expanded upon in the Christian apocrypha, in the Talmud, in Kabbalah, and in Islamic folklore. Other spirits are mentioned in various grimoires, such as Olympian spirits and planetary spirits (see page 78). Pagan ceremonial magicians might invoke Pagan deities, elemental spirits, or other entities.

In CM, rituals are performed that force angels or deities to appear through the use of evocation, magical tools, symbols, names of God, and other words of power. These entities, once evoked, are instructed to fulfill the will of the magician. While in folk magic, one might use a dowsing rod to find treasure, in CM, one invokes an angel or demon with power to find treasure and commands them to do so.

Symbols and Sigils

We've explored planetary and zodiacal symbols, but CM goes beyond that. Each angel, demon, and spirit has one or more symbols that can be used to invoke them. There are also planetary pentacles, seals, and shapes. These are both invocatory and protective. For example, the protective "Seal of Solomon" is a seven-pointed star surrounded by angelic names with planetary and other symbols placed within it. Ritual and invocation rely heavily on the use of such symbols. A "seal" might also *seal* a being into place, forcing it to do the will of the magician.

We briefly explored sigils in chapter 4. There are several techniques by which a sigil might be created—number squares are one powerful example. The technique of drawing connected lines, such as on number squares, can be used by drawing on other "maps," and other techniques are possible as well. Sigils (in CM and elsewhere) are used for invocation but also for magical intention. For example, you could spell a word and use numerology (see page 74) to create a number square sigil from it. The sigil pours your intention into the magic. The combination of symbols and sigils helps create the ritual, empower it, and protect it, and then imposes the intention onto it.

Protection and Precision

One characteristic of CM is that protection from the entities invoked is always present. Even if no one *says* that the circle protects you, it is always implied. In *The Golden Dawn*, for example, Israeli Regardie says, *"At all times complete the circle of the place before commencing an invocation."*

Rituals must be performed precisely. Tools must be made or purchased at the correct planetary hour and when they are "virgin" (new and never before used). Once made, they are blessed according to precise instructions by a magician who has prepared themselves according to similarly strict guidance.

These rules imply that the magic will not work without precision in every step of the magical operation, but they also imply that ritual and the entities invoked are dangerous, and only by performing every step with the utmost care is it safe to proceed.

⟡⊢ MEET ⊣⟡
DONALD MICHAEL KRAIG

Donald Michael Kraig (1951–2014) was an occultist, author, and editor. In his book *Modern Magick*, Don blended ceremonial magic with Neo-Pagan ideas; he may have been the first to do so, and he sought to break down the walls between the two.

He took an obscure subject and described it in plain English. He wrote about magic (including an excellent book on sex magic), tarot, and tantra, was a hypnotherapist and a professional keyboard player, and held a degree in philosophy from UCLA. He died of pancreatic cancer at age 62.

FROM ANTIQUITY TO TODAY

As we've seen, magic has existed since antiquity, and recognizable CM goes back more than 700 years. In that period of time, there have naturally been a number of variations on CM. Let's look at some key ones more closely.

MAGIC IN ANTIQUITY

As you may recall, Hermes Trismegistus called magic one of the "three parts of wisdom." Writings attributed to Hermes include astrological and talisman magic and also offer lists of sympathetic magical correspondences.

The *Greek Magical Papyri*, a collection of documents dating back to about 100 BCE, shows continuity with later ceremonial magic and includes a wide range of spells, some of which resemble folk magic, and some which are more ritualistic. Prayers, amulets, invoking demons, and many other techniques are included.

In this period, both Jewish and Egyptian magic thrived. Magic was and is forbidden by Jewish law, but evidence that it thrived is plentiful in the form of papyri, amulets, and incantation bowls (bowls inscribed with a magical spell). Egyptian magic also involved amulets, as well as temple rituals and even invocatory tattoos.

THE GRIMOIRE TRADITION

The grimoire tradition (see page 119) is also known as Solomonic or Renaissance magic, and tends to claim authority from the Biblical King Solomon. It is primarily goetic, meaning that demons might be evoked and specific, worldly goals are assumed. For example, even though *The Sworn Book of Honorius* speaks of piety and prayer, it's as willing to invoke demons as angels, and it lists operations such as "To open locks," "To cause discord," "To have wealth," "To cure any sickness," and "To kill anyone."

Grimoires borrow heavily from Jewish magic, mix in traditional Christianity, and draw on a long history of magic in Egypt, Greece, and the ancient Middle East.

ENOCHIAN MAGIC

In Enochian magic (originally called Angelic magic), angels are invoked using "calls" in the "Angelic language" in a carefully erected temple. The system is incredibly complex and has even been compared to magical brain surgery!

John Dee was the court astronomer/astrologer to Elizabeth I. (He was also her spy, code name 007.) He was an occultist, alchemist, and Hermeticist. In 1582, he met Edward Kelley, a gifted medium (some say a charlatan). Over a period of several years, they worked together, Dee invoking angels and Kelley channeling them. Dee wrote down everything told to him by the angels.

Dee's notes start with planetary magic (the "Heptarchia" or "Heptarchia Mystica"), not unlike other Renaissance magic. Next was dictated the legendary Book of Enoch, given to the Biblical Enoch in the heavens (hence "Enochian"). This book provides a system of magic, as well as the "Angelic language." Last to be dictated was a sort of magical map of the Earth, divided into four sections called "Watchtowers."

THE HERMETIC ORDER OF THE GOLDEN DAWN

The Hermetic Order of the Golden Dawn was a secret society structured in lodges with a training program moving initiates from the Outer to the Inner Order. The ceremonial magic of the group was Hermetic in philosophy, using Kabbalah, tarot, astrology, grimoires, and (in the higher grades) Enochian magic.

The Isis-Urania Temple of the Golden Dawn was founded in 1888 by William Westcott, S. L. MacGregor Mathers, and Dr. W. R. Woodman. Golden Dawn members included some of the world's most famous magicians, such as Moina Mathers (Mathers's wife), Arthur Edward Waite, Pamela Colman Smith, Aleister Crowley, Dion Fortune (in the offshoot Alpha et Omega), and William Butler Yeats. Soon it had hundreds of members.

By 1914, it was all over. Given the intensity of the many personalities involved and the mind-altering work they were doing, it's not surprising that the Golden Dawn split apart acrimoniously. Yet from its seeds, magnificent trees grew.

⋙⋙⋙ MEET ⊢⋖⋗
ALEISTER CROWLEY

Edward Alexander (Aleister) Crowley (1875–1947) was an English occultist, ceremonial magician, and author. In 1904, while in Cairo, he was contacted by Aiwass, a messenger of the Egyptian god Horus, who dictated *The Book of the Law*—the core religious text of Thelema, the Pagan/ magical religion Crowley founded.

Crowley subsequently cofounded the A∴A∴, a CM order based in Golden Dawn and Thelema. He introduced the spelling of "magick" and created the Thoth tarot. His book *Magick in Theory and Practice* is considered a masterpiece. He was called the "wickedest man in the world" for his practice of sex magic and open bisexuality. Crowley remains one of the most influential thinkers, writers, and creators in occult history. Rejected by many today for his misogyny and racism, his magical ideas still permeate occultism.

THE ORDO TEMPLI ORIENTIS (OTO) AND THELEMA

The Ordo Templi Orientis (OTO) was an occult organization based in Freemasonry, founded sometime around 1904. Aleister Crowley joined in 1910 and was soon in a leadership position. He rewrote the initiation rituals, shifted the basis of the OTO to Thelema, and wrote the Gnostic Mass, which became the OTO's central ritual.

The Book of the Law by Crowley is famous for this quote: "Do what thou wilt shall be the whole of the Law." While this is easily understood as libertine and amoral, Thelema expects each person to find their "True Will," their destiny, which brings them in harmony with nature. So "what thou wilt" is acting in accordance with your True Will, not with whatever strikes your fancy.

The OTO remains a vital occult organization with dozens of chapters throughout the world.

THE SOCIETY OF INNER LIGHT (SIL)

In 1927, Dion Fortune joined, and quickly took over, the Christian Mystic Lodge of the Theosophical Society. The group split from both Theosophy and Alpha et Omega, was renamed a couple of times, became the Fraternity of Inner Light, and today is known as the Society of Inner Light (SIL).

Over time, SIL moved further and further from Golden Dawn–style CM, and it now rejects goetia and practical magic entirely. Its initiations and ritual magic are uniquely its own. SIL is focused on rituals that guide one through the Hermetic Kabbalah for the purpose of expansion of consciousness and evolution.

OTHER MAGICAL GROUPS

When internal strife caused a split from Mathers's leadership, the Golden Dawn broke apart like a seedpod, spreading new groups far and wide. The Matherses remained in Alpha et Omega (the original offshoot). Arthur Waite formed the Fellowship of the Rosy Cross, which was focused on Christian Mysticism. More occult-oriented former members, including William Butler Yeats and Israel Regardie, created Stella Matutina.

Paul Foster Case, an author and expert on tarot, Kabbalah, and the occult, left Alpha et Omega, eventually forming Builders of the Adytum (BOTA). Case was unhappy with the inclusion of Enochian material in Golden Dawn rites. He thought the rituals were dangerous because they have little in the way of protection or safeguards built in.

The OTO, SIL, and BOTA are just a few of the current magical groups with a direct or indirect lineage from the Golden Dawn.

CEREMONIAL MAGIC TOOL KIT

The tools for CM vary widely, depending on the grimoire, school of thought, and techniques used. Given the nature of CM, the tools are often made according to elaborate and precise directions. The following is a basic list of Golden Dawn tools. Refer to *The Golden Dawn* or *Modern Magick* for instructions on the construction and consecration of each (see page 159).

ELEMENTAL TOOLS are an Air Dagger (a double-edged blade with a T-shaped hilt, a yellow handle, and certain symbols painted on it), a Fire Wand (red with yellow, and an acorn-shaped tip), a Water Chalice (a stemmed blue goblet with symbols on it), and an Earth Pentacle (a disk with a hexagram on it, painted with the colors of Malkut; see page 108).

WORKING TOOLS include a sword, an additional dagger (for use in ritual, rather than for representing an element), a "Lotus wand" (rainbow painted, with a lotus-flower tip), other wands for specific rituals, a symbol of the "rose cross," a robe to wear, various incenses and an incense burner, candles, and a table to use as an altar.

IN *THE KEY OF SOLOMON THE KING*, the following tools are illustrated: the Knife with the White Hilt, the Knife with the Black Hilt, the Scimitar, the Short Lance, the Dagger, the Sickle, the Peniard (a kind of sword), the Staff, the Wand, the Magical Sword, and the Burin (an engraving tool).

CHAOS MAGIC

Although chaos magic didn't appear until the 1970s, it is rooted in the theories and techniques of artist and occultist Austin Osman Spare, an early member of A∴A∴. Chaos magic seeks to strip away unnecessary dogmas and rituals from occult work, and it requires no specific magical tools. It is practical, concerned with achieving real-world results—jobs, love, health, etc. In chaos magic, "nothing is true; everything is permitted." The origin of the phrase "chaos magic" is not clear, but "chaos" is used to mean a cosmic source, or "God," not something chaotic.

In a way, Spare went full circle back to the simplicity of folk magic, just as Gerald Gardner (see page 27) did (although Spare didn't like Gardner and didn't want a religion). Chaos magic acknowledges no external reality. In chaos magic, you're not invoking real angels; you're pouring energy into the invocation, which can create a seemingly independent entity called a "servitor." Any technique, from any system, can be used, since it's the energy and belief of the magician that are the only reality.

THE WORK OF THE MAGICIAN

You might be wondering, what do magicians actually do? Their work falls into several large buckets: work on the mind or self of the magician, work on the construction and consecration of tools of magic, creation of ritual space, and the invocation and evocation of angels, demons, and other beings. (Naturally, it's all done in accordance with proper planetary days and hours.) Let's look more closely.

INNER WORK

Magicians work on themselves for a number of reasons. First, to empower themselves to do magic. This includes exercises to improve visualization and concentration, as well as body/mind work such as postures or breathing exercises, and specific exercises in ceremonial techniques, such as vibration (see page 133) and pathworking (see page 115).

Second, inner work is sometimes the purpose of the magic itself. Thelema sees "knowledge and conversation of the Holy Guardian Angel" as a key purpose of magic, which leads to "crossing the Abyss." (In chapter 6, I noted most Kabbalists think crossing the Abyss is impossible in life; Thelema is the exception.) While evocation and invocation are crucial, so are inner exploration, moving through the Tree of Life, and consciousness expansion.

Finally, inner work is considered part of the Great Work of transforming the world: "As above, so below." As we transform ourselves, we move a tiny piece of the entire universe forward. The Society of Inner Light (SIL; see page 129) considers this the core work of magic.

THE VIBRATORY FORMULA

The vibratory formula is a vocal and mental technique used through-out CM. It is needed for vibrating names of power and invocation and is used in the most basic ritual that all ceremonial magicians learn: the Lesser Banishing Ritual of the Pentagram (LBRP). Vibration should be done standing, if possible, just as deep diaphragm singing should be.

INSTRUCTIONS:

1. Inhale deeply. While doing so, visualize a brilliant white light entering your lungs.

2. Intone a vowel sound (such as "oooh") while releasing the breath and the bright color. Continue toning until all air is fully expelled. Your voice is louder and probably higher than normal. The goal is to experience a vibration or tingling in your chest as you intone.

3. Continue experimenting with steps 1 and 2, changing the shape of your mouth, your posture, and the tone of your voice until you discover your personal magical voice.

4. Once you have mastered creating vibration in this way, repeat the exercise on page 110. This time, vibrate each Hebrew word. You'll begin with bright white light on inhalation, but on exhalation, use the color of the sephirah, while attempting to feel the vibration in the corresponding body part. For example, for Chokmah, you'll expel a gray color while vibrating the left side of your face.

CREATING TOOLS OF MAGIC

Some of the working tools for ceremonial magic (see page 130) can be purchased, but most are made. Often, it's a combination of the two: you might purchase a dagger and then paint the handle yellow and inscribe it with the required symbols and letters. Other tools created by a magician include sigils, amulets, talismans, and magic squares, all previously discussed.

Once a tool has been made, it must be consecrated. This is generally done within a consecrated ritual space (a magic circle). The consecration includes asperging (sprinkling with water) and censing (passing through incense). Grimoires show consecrations specific to each tool and its purpose.

CREATION OF RITUAL SPACE

Ceremonial magicians cast magic circles for protection. They may also create spaces such as triangles, into which demons might be invoked—if you don't want to be in the same space as some critter, you stand in the circle and invoke the entity into the triangle, which you've set up outside the circle. The ritual space is used for all consecrations, but of course tools are needed to create the space, so you'd create tools, consecrate them, and then create the full magic circle before any deeper or more complex rituals are done. The Lesser Banishing Ritual of the Pentagram (LBRP) is a starting point for ritual creation. Ceremonial magicians learn it, and then learn the Lesser Invoking Ritual of the Pentagram (LIRP), the greater versions of these, and the corresponding rituals of the Hexagram.

INVOCATION AND EVOCATION

This is the core work of CM, and everything else is done in service of it. The tools, the meditations, and the ritual spaces are all for the purpose of invoking various entities. Mostly, the word "invocation" is used, but many magicians distinguish between "invocation" into one's own body (possession) and "evocation" into ritual space. Usually CM is about evocation, although both occur.

The trained, prepared magician, at the proper time, with proper consecrated tools, sets up a ritual space that will protect them from the entity to be evoked. Using visualization, sigils, seals, and vibration, the magician calls forth the entity to be present and then instructs it as to why it has been called. After properly releasing it, the ritual space is carefully dismantled.

THE CRUCIBLE
OF CEREMONIAL
MAGIC

Having read this far, we can see that everything in Western and Middle Eastern occult history ended up incorporated into the flowering of CM in the Renaissance. (Look again at the timeline on page 154.)

- ◆ Heinrich Cornelius Agrippa, in particular, incorporates virtually all preceding occult streams: Gnosticism, Hermeticism, Neoplatonism, astrology, theurgy, goetia, Kabbalah, and the study of angels are all part of his *Three Books of Occult Philosophy*.
- ◆ In the Hermetic Order of the Golden Dawn, everything that Agrippa incorporated remains present, but Enochian magic, magical lodges, Rosicrucianism, and Theosophy are also included. The Golden Dawn treated Western occultism like a funnel and believed itself to be the pinnacle of all such magical traditions and studies.
- ◆ The Golden Dawn was a crucible, an alchemical furnace that took disparate elements and transformed them into something new. Not *one* something, as in alchemy, but *many* somethings. Virtually everything in the Western occult today was touched, directly or indirectly, by the Golden Dawn, including Thelema, chaos magic, and Wicca.

It is common for a Wiccan or Neo-Pagan to think that CM is ridiculously complex and can easily be ignored. Many Wiccans, including me, don't practice CM in any formal way. But the fact is, the magic we *do* practice was influenced by CM, and a study of the subject deepens one's practice— whatever that practice happens to be.

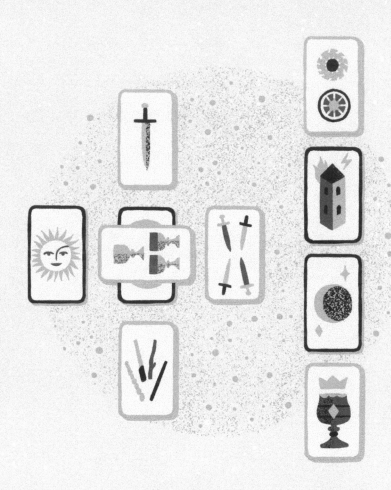

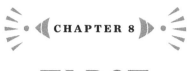

CHAPTER 8

TAROT

Tarot cards are a specific type of cards used in the occult for divination, meditation, and magic. A deck consists of 78 cards, divided into the 22 fully illustrated cards of the Major Arcana (the "trumps") and the 56 cards of the Minor Arcana. The minors are similar to modern playing cards, consisting of four suits, each numbered 1 through 10, plus four "court cards." (Playing cards dropped the Knight from the court and renamed the Page to "Jack.") Minors may just have pips, indicating number and suit, but since the twentieth century, they are usually fully illustrated. Occult cards that don't meet the definition of tarot are called "oracle cards."

The history of tarot is pretty well-known, yet pseudo-histories remain prevalent. People think that tarot is thousands of years old, that it originated in Egypt, and that it survived from the ancient Egyptian Book of Thoth. Or that tarot was originally a secret encoding of occult knowledge—that during the Inquisition, when writing about such things was dangerous, the mysteries were recorded in pictorial form.

Many occultists believe the correspondence between Kabbalah and tarot (more on that shortly) was there from the beginning, and that tarot is originally a Jewish mystery. A popular recent belief is that tarot originated with the Romani people. Indeed, some people (some Romani and some not) think that the use of tarot represents cultural appropriation. (A Roma diviner—a *drabardi*—might use tarot or other cards, but it's not a native part of Roma culture.)

However, none of these theories are true. We're not sure where modern playing cards come from, but they were probably brought to Europe from the Islamic world by soldiers returning from the Crusades. Tarot, though, derives from *tarocchi*, an Italian Renaissance game of the upper classes, similar to bridge, which combined playing cards with a set of trumps illustrated with figures like the Fool and the Devil, familiar from carnival parades. The first known tarocchi deck, the Visconti-Sforza, dates to the mid-fifteenth century. It took a while for the number of trumps and their characters to become consistent. Here they remained, a big gaming deck, until the late eighteenth century.

Then, in a short period of time, Éliphas Lévi (see page 120) connected tarot to the Kabbalah and to Hebrew. Meanwhile, different writers linked tarot to ancient Egypt and to the Romani (who were thought to be from Egypt), while yet another writer linked them to divination. All of this meant that when the occult revival occurred, tarot was incorporated into the Golden Dawn system and stayed along for the ride thereafter.

A. E. Waite and Pamela Colman Smith (see pages 147 and 144) introduced the first major innovation when they illustrated all 78 cards in the Rider-Waite deck. (Rider was the publisher; today it's more frequently called Waite-Smith, Rider-Waite-Smith, or RWS for short.) As mentioned earlier, Aleister Crowley created the Thoth tarot, making numerous small changes. Today, almost every tarot deck is a variation on either RWS (usually) or Thoth.

Tarot is now more popular than ever before. GoFundMe and various self-publishing sites have allowed a profusion of innovative magical artists to create a vast array of tarot decks in every possible artistic style, for every occult area of study, and for every kind of human being. Decks are Kabbalistic or not, astrological or not, numerological or not. Decks have been created for queer readers, young readers, movie buffs, art lovers, cat people, and more. It is a great time to be a student of tarot!

UNDERSTANDING TAROT

If you fall in love with tarot, you'll want to study it in depth. You'll find several great starting points on page 160. In the meantime, let's look at the terminology, structure, and occult connections of tarot, in order to get an overview of its place in the occult and, potentially, in your life.

THE MAJORS AND THE MINORS

As we've seen, tarot was originally a pack of cards (the Minor Arcana) with a set of trumps (the Major Arcana) added. The two sets of cards are treated differently.

The 22 Majors are numbered 0 through 21. The Majors are understood to be mystical and deal with important matters. As a whole, the majors are variously thought of as a hero's journey; the soul's journey through incarnation; the paths of the Tree of Life; the movement of fate through one's life; or simply major life events. While each trump is read as an individual card, they are also a sequence, experienced in order and in relation to one another, so that, for example, the placement of the Fool (trump 0) at the beginning or end is considered a significant decision. There are some decks and some spreads (see page 146) that use only Major Arcana.

The 56 Minors are numbered 1 through 10, followed by Page, Knight, Queen, and King in each of four suits. The Minors are treated as providing ordinary information. Things predicted by the Minor Arcana are not considered as life-altering as those predicted by the Majors.

LEARNING TAROT

There are different schools of thought in approaching the learning process. Some teachers want you to just be with the pictures on each card and develop your own understanding before ever reading a book. Having taught tarot for many years, I think memorization, while difficult at first, will free up your inner psychic. Get a good beginner book (see page 160) or start with the booklet that came with your deck.

YOU'LL NEED:

A tarot deck and booklet   A journal
Index cards and paperclips

INSTRUCTIONS:

1. Create a set of flash cards for your deck: on 78 index cards, write the upright and reversed meaning of each card, then gently clip it to the back of the card. This will allow you to study from either direction (look at the card and remember what it means, or look at the meaning and remember which card it is).
2. Study daily and get "off book" as soon as you can.
3. Keep a card journal and draw a card each morning. Write down the card and what you think it predicts for the day. In the evening, note how it connected to your day.
4. Read one or three cards for small events frequently: *Will I like this movie? Who's at the door?* A quick cut and glance at a card will do. This can be journaled as well.

With these simple exercises—memorization, journaling, and practice—you'll soon develop comfort and knowledge that will expand beyond "beginner" into lifelong learning.

The Suits and the Numbers

The four tarot suits are Wands (sometimes called batons, rods, or staffs), Swords, Cups, and Pentacles (sometimes called discs or coins). We've encountered these before, as tools of witchcraft and ceremonial magic. Just as in magic, these tools/suits correspond to the four elements of Fire (Wands), Air (Swords), Water (Cups), and Earth (Pentacles). The meaning of the elements is consistent throughout Western occultism, whether in astrology, alchemy, or tarot. In some occult systems, there is a fifth element, Spirit. If Spirit is used as an element, it corresponds to the Majors.

Similarly, the numbers can be understood by knowledge of numbers in the occult, using your study of numerology, astrology, and Kabbalah. There is at least one book (*Numerology: Key to the Tarot* by Sandor Konraad) that interprets the cards based primarily on their Pythagorean numerology (see chapter 4).

While each card has an individual and specific meaning, enormous insight is gained simply by looking at suit and number. For example, regardless of what else the Ace of Wands is, it's always also a beginning (one) of Fire (Wands).

The Tarot Court

There are a bunch of people running around your tarot deck. The court cards generally represent people, although they can be interpreted in other ways, such as inner qualities. Pages are often messages, and Knights often represent movement. Figuring out who the people are can be a challenge to a beginner.

Traditionally, Pages are children of any gender, Knights are young men, Queens are women, and Kings are older men or authority figures. Newer tarot decks interpret the cards with less rigidity about gender, and many purposely present a queer point of view. For example, in the Next World Tarot deck, the Queen of Pentacles is bearded and appears male (all the court cards in this deck are described with gender-neutral pronouns).

⟡— MEET —⟡
PAMELA COLMAN SMITH

Pamela Colman "Pixie" Smith (1878–1951) was an artist, writer, and publisher, most famous for illustrating the RWS deck. Born in London to American parents, she grew up in Jamaica and Brooklyn, New York.

By age 21, she was orphaned and living in London, where she became part of a bohemian set that included W. B. Yeats and Bram Stoker, of *Dracula* fame. She joined the Golden Dawn in 1901, where she met Waite (see page 147). She was paid a flat fee (and not much) for illustrating Waite's tarot deck. Although she'd had early success as an artist, work became scarce. She died in obscurity. Historians typically don't speculate on orientation, but Smith lived for 40 years with Nora Lake and willed her estate to her "friend."

∞∞

KABBALAH AND THE TAROT

As we've learned, the Kabbalah has 22 paths, corresponding to the 22 letters of the Hebrew alphabet. There are 10 sephirot, each with four emanations corresponding to the four elements. The tarot has 22 Majors, and 10 numbered Minors in four suits. Once Éliphas Lévi pointed out this correspondence, it was hard to ignore, and it became the basis for every tarot deck produced during the occult revival. These decks, especially RWS, are the foundation for almost all newer decks, so even if a tarot creator isn't a student of Kabbalah and isn't consciously inserting Kabbalistic meaning into the cards, anything based on Waite-Smith or Crowley (or Lévi himself, or Paul Foster Case, or Dion Fortune, etc.) is inherently Kabbalistic.

It's important to understand that tarot as it comes to us today is a product of the occult revival, especially the Golden Dawn and its many offshoots. The illustrations and interpretations are rooted in Hermetic Kabbalah and in its many correspondences, including to astrology, the elements, numerology, and so on.

CHOOSING A TAROT DECK

A tarot deck can be a true companion, so you want to choose wisely. While a deck must appeal to your aesthetics, a lot more goes into the decision. Don't expect your first deck to be your last. As you're learning tarot, you're also learning how you respond to the cards, and that will inform your choices.

Start with a deck that many books refer to, such as RWS or something similar. Observe your interactions with it as you handle and lay out the cards; take note of what you like and dislike about working with the deck. If possible, borrow a friend's deck as well.

Ask yourself these questions about the deck you want:

→ Do you respond to lots of detail, finding yourself falling into parts of a picture, noticing different elements on different occasions? Or do you feel most intuitive with a lack of detail, letting your imagination run free?

→ Do text and information on a card help ground you, or do they get in the way?

→ Do you have other occult interests that might inform your choice, such as Kabbalah or astrology? If so, look for a deck that highlights those parts of tarot.

→ Do you have personal considerations, such as needing to see nonbinary people, people of color, disabled people, or no people at all on your cards?

→ How will you use the deck (see page 151)? For meditation, you might prefer more static images, while for prediction, movement can be more helpful.

→ How does a deck feel in your hands? If you have very small hands or have arthritis, some decks will be too large and feel uncomfortable.

To view a variety of decks and their illustrations, check out the websites listed on page 160.

Divination, Synchronicity, and Meaning

"Divination" is the art of seeing the future or hidden truths about the present or past. It is considered a more accurate and more respectful term than "fortune-telling." Tarot is a tool of divination—there are many such tools, including astrology, runes, tea leaves, and scrying.

Carl Jung coined the word "synchronicity" for "meaningful coincidence." We don't necessarily know how or why a synchronous occurrence is meaningful, but we perceive that it is. Synchronicity depends on randomness; if nothing is left to chance, no coincidence can occur. All divination has an element of randomness, and this allows synchronicity to be generated.

In tarot, that randomness is the shuffle. Since you don't know what card you'll pick, the one that is picked in response to your question or wisdom-seeking is the one that is meaningful.

Tarot Spreads

A tarot reading is typically done in a "spread" or "layout." That is, each card has a meaning, but so does its position. A spread often looks like something that indicates the meaning of the cards, so past-present-future will read from left to right, just as a narrative would. The top of a spread might be a goal, while the bottom might be the "base" of an issue.

The most popular spread is certainly the Celtic Cross (see the illustration on page 138), introduced to the world by A. E. Waite's *The Pictorial Key to the Tarot* in 1910. It has a lot of nuance, combining prediction (past, present, future, and outcome cards) with analysis of the current situation (covering, crossing, foundation, and environment cards), and adding in psychology (self-image, hopes, and fears). It's definitely worth learning!

◇⟶ MEET ⟵◇
A. E. WAITE

Arthur Edward Waite (1857–1942) was a poet, writer, and mystic born in New York and raised in England. After his younger sister died when he was just 17, he turned from Catholicism to spiritualism, mysticism, and Theosophy, eventually becoming a Rosicrucian, Freemason, and member of the Golden Dawn, before forming the Fellowship of the Rosy Cross.

Waite is most famous for the tarot deck he cocreated with Pamela Colman Smith. Among his instructions to Smith, he said to "follow very carefully the astrological significance of each suit as it is influenced by different zodiacal signs." Waite's other claim to fame is in earning the enmity of Aleister Crowley (see page 128), who cast him as the villain Arthwaite in his novel *Moonchild*.

TAROT VARIATIONS

Tarot itself has innumerable variations because there are so many decks out there—well over a thousand on the market right now. Most are based on RWS. That said, many decks are modeled after Aleister Crowley's Thoth deck, and so are influenced by Thelema, with its unique, innovative, and artistic take on the occult. There are also a few decks from other occult schools of thought. There are also non-tarot decks. Lenormand cards have taken off in the last few years, and the variety of available oracle decks is immense. Let's look at each of these more closely.

Occult Tarot

The work of A. E. Waite and Pamela Colman Smith in the RWS deck is mysterious yet accessible and contains both Kabbalistic and Christian elements; the Tree of Life and the name of God are hidden in several cards. Waite's focus was on the Major Arcana. Scholars think he left Smith to devise the 56 Minor illustrations entirely on her own. The RWS is the most popular deck in the world, with over 100 million copies in print.

The BOTA tarot deck is a variation on RWS by Paul Foster Case (see page 129). Case was convinced that Waite made his deck deliberately obscure and included mistakes, and this was a "correction."

Some decks are based directly on the teachings of Éliphas Lévi (see page 120), combining tarot, Kabbalah, and the mysteries of ancient Egypt. Two such decks are the Papus Tarot (which is brightly colored, with Egyptian-style occult imagery and pips for the Minors), and the Oswald Wirth Tarot Deck. To a student of Lévi's, Wirth's deck looks more traditional.

The Society of Inner Light (see page 129) published the Dion Fortune Tarot. Though not created by Fortune, it is based on her teachings and is intended for use in meditation.

The Thoth Tarot

For the beginning student of tarot, Thoth presents both challenges and advantages. Created by Aleister Crowley and Lady Frieda Harris, the associated book (*The Book of Thoth*) is dense and can be hard to follow. On the other hand, the inclusion of signs and planets on almost every card gives astrological information, and Hebrew letters on each card provide insight for Kabbalists. Every card, including the Minors, has a name, which is great for the beginner. ("Abundance" is objectively easier to understand than "Three of Cups.")

Crowley both disliked Waite personally and disagreed with much of his work. The two interpreted the astrology, Kabbalah, and mysticism of the tarot differently. It's inarguable that the RWS is now "standard" in tarot, so the Thoth differences can be confusing. In the Major Arcana, some names are changed. The confusing ones are Lust instead of Strength, Adjustment instead of Justice, Art instead of Temperance, and the Æon instead of Judgement. The other thing that can be tricky is that the Page in Thoth is the Princess, while Knight and King are Prince and Knight.

REVERSALS

When you shuffle cards randomly, some will be upside down. In tarot, an upside-down card is called a "reversal" and is given a different meaning than the same card upright. Most reversals are negative, although sometimes a reversal softens the blow of a negative card or enhances a positive card.

Some people don't read reversals and "fix" cards that come up reversed as they lay out a spread. Some do this to simplify reading— it's already 78 meanings to memorize, after all! Some say that the reversed meaning is inherent in the card, and it's up to the intuition of the reader to uncover which way to read. On the other hand, more information is more information, and position is one way that synchronicity tells you the nature of the card at this moment.

The Motherpeace Tarot, a feminist deck created in 1983, took the tarot world by storm. The cards in this deck are round. Some readers understood this to mean there were no reversals. By contrast, others found that the shape allowed for even more nuance in reading reversals, as a card could be at any angle of a circle, which subtly altered the meaning of the card.

LENORMAND CARDS

An entirely different divination system that uses cards, Lenormand goes back to a French parlor game of the late eighteenth century. The deck used for divination is technically the *Petit Jeu Lenormand*; it consists of 36 cards with simple symbols that are strung together in spreads that form narratives.

In Lenormand, ships are "travel," clovers are "luck," and coffins are "grief"—the straightforward meanings appeal to many people, and this system has become quite popular. Readers who want to work with intuition, deep insight, meditation, and underlying causes will prefer tarot, but some prefer Lenormand for details of exactly what may happen.

◇—⊢ MEET ⊢—◇ RACHEL POLLACK

Rachel Grace Pollack (1945–) is a prolific and award-winning author of both nonfiction and fiction, including comic books, as well as a renowned expert on the tarot. She has created three tarot decks of her own and written companion guides to several decks.

As the author of *Seventy-Eight Degrees of Wisdom*, she is the creator of *the* modern classic on the subject. She's also written about the Kabbalah. Pollack was raised an Orthodox Jew in her birthplace of Brooklyn, New York. A trans woman, Pollack has written about trans issues and created one of the first trans characters in comic books (Coagula of *Doom Patrol*).

Oracle Decks

The term "oracle deck" is used for any card deck, regardless of theme, content, or number of cards, that is used for meditative or divination purposes. There are hundreds on the market. They can be used alone or in conjunction with tarot or other divination tools. For example, the Wild Unknown Animal Spirit Deck is designed as a companion to the Wild Unknown Tarot. Some themes of oracle decks are goddesses, Mayan magic, Celtic trees, sacred geometry, tantra, the African diaspora, Indigenous American ways, and love.

USING THE TAROT

We can break the use of the tarot into two broad areas: inner work and outer work. Think of meditation, self-exploration, and psychological insight as "inner," and think of prediction for yourself or others, as well as magic, as "outer." Outer work has real-world results and inner work does not. Tarot is useful for both.

PREDICTION

Whenever we have a card in the spread position of "future," we're predicting. Predictive tarot exists on a continuum of more or less psychological, more or less practical. For example, in a past-present-future spread, you might use tarot to explore fears of the past and opportunities of the future, or you might be very mundane, predicting job offers, chance meetings, and financial outcomes. The tarot is flexible enough to do either or both.

Since the position of a card in a spread tells you what that card is addressing, and since there are a virtually infinite number of spreads, tarot can predict anything. The Celtic Cross, for example, has a "crossing" card, telling the querent (the person receiving the reading) what is at odds with them. This could be anything from a psychological state to a toxic boss.

Prediction can be for yourself, others, or world events. Tarot readers differ on who to read for. Some read only for themselves; some never for themselves. Reading can be for friends and acquaintances or can be done professionally.

PSYCHOLOGY AND SELF-EXPLORATION

Many people use the tarot only for themselves, never reading on behalf of others. To them, tarot is a tool of self-exploration. There are a number of ways of doing this. Most popular is a "card of the day"—drawing a single card to start your day to bring an understanding of who you are and what your challenges will be today. Another is periodic readings, such as monthly and/or annually (perhaps on New Year's Eve or your birthday) and at any turning point.

MEDITATION

A tarot card can be a powerful meditation image. You might use it as a purely visual gateway to meditation—gazing at it as one might gaze at a mandala. Doing this also allows you to internalize the energies of the card. For instance, meditating on Justice might be a way of bringing fairness, balance, and justice into your life.

A card can also be a trigger for a Kabbalistic or planetary meditation. For example, the World corresponds to the path between Malkut and Yesod (see page 115); you could use the World in meditation while working on that path.

Tarot meditation can emerge spontaneously or deliberately. A card might appear troublesome or significant during a reading; you can then use it for meditation. Or you could deliberately ask the cards, "What do I need to meditate on right now?" and the card drawn becomes your meditation object.

TAROT MAGIC

Tarot cards can be used as part of a spell in a number of ways. They can be used as sympathetic objects (see page 3). A card can represent a quality, an element, an outcome, a sephirah, etc. A spread can also be set so that the outcome you seek is prearranged—that is, instead of doing a reading and learning the future by turning up a card in the position for the future, you determine in advance which card will turn up by placing it in the correct position, basically "stacking the deck." For such a spell, I read out loud, stating each piece of the reading and outcome as part of the magic.

CONNECTING
THE DOTS

As we come to the end of our journey through the occult, we land at tarot. We can see that tarot holds a connection to the areas of Western occultism in every chapter we've previously explored.

- ◆ Tarot is connected to folk magic and witchcraft through divination traditions.
- ◆ Although not strictly a part of Wicca, tarot is used by most Wiccans.
- ◆ Tarot is connected to numerology: the cards are numbered, and the numbers have meaning.
- ◆ Like virtually anything in occultism, tarot has a connection to the elements and to the planets.
- ◆ Through Hermetics, tarot, astrology, alchemy, and Kabbalah are all interconnected. Tarot cards are on the Tree of Life, are used in ceremonial magic, and are used in pathworking.

Tarot is a Western practice and connects to Western occultism. Divination exists in other cultures, of course, from African bone reading to the Chinese I Ching. And, as you might expect, these divination systems connect to the internal beliefs and the occultism of their cultures.

Finally, we've journeyed through this rich subject, its history, its practices, and its rainbow of variations. All that's left for you is to continue your explorations.

OCCULT TIMELINE

Late Antiquity

200-475 CE

PHILOSOPHIES
Gnosticism
Hermeticism
Neoplatonism

PRACTICES
Astrology
Alchemy
Theurgy
Goetia

PUBLICATIONS
The Hermetica
Greek Magical Papyri
Jewish Magical Papyri

Middle Ages

476-1299 CE

ORGANIZATION
Trade Guilds

PRACTICES
Kabbalah
Angelology

PUBLICATION
The Zohar

Renaissance

1300-1599 CE

PRACTICES
Enochian Magic
The Grimoire Tradition

PUBLICATION
Three Books of Occult Philosophy

PEOPLE
John Dee and Edward Kelly

Cornelius Heinrich Agrippa

Enlightenment

1685-1815 CE

SCHOOL OF THOUGHT
The Rosicrucians

ORGANIZATION
First Freemason
Grand Lodge

PRACTICE
Lodge Magic

PUBLICATION
The Magus

PERSON
Swedenborg

Occult Revival

1840-1901 CE

PHILOSOPHY
Theosophy

ORGANIZATION
Hermetic Order of the
Golden Dawn

PUBLICATION
The Secret Doctrine

PEOPLE
Éliphas Lévi
Madame Helena
Blavatasky

Modernity

1902 CE-present

ORGANIZATIONS
Builders of the Adytum
The OTO
Fraternity of the Inner Light
Sangreal Sodality
The A∴A∴
Orde Aurum Solios
Typhonian Order

PHILOSOPHIES
Chaos Magic
Wicca
Neopaganism
Thelema

PEOPLE
Dion Fortune
Aleister Crowley
William Gray
Gerald Gardner
Austin Osman Square
Kenneth Grant

Further Reading & Exploration

CHAPTER 1: FOLK MAGIC

The Complete Book of Incense, Oils & Brews by Scott Cunningham (Llewellyn, 1989)

Encyclopedia of 5,000 Spells by Judika Illes (HarperOne, 2011)

Real Magic: An Introductory Treatise on the Basic Principles of Yellow Magic by Isaac Bonewits (Red Wheel, 1989)

Throwing the Bones: How to Foretell the Future with Bones, Shells, and Nuts by Catherine Yronwode (Lucky Mojo Curio Company, 2012)

Voodoo and Afro-Caribbean Paganism by Lilith Dorsey (Citadel, 2005)

CHAPTER 2: WITCHCRAFT

Drawing Down the Moon: Witches, Druids, Goddess-Worshippers, and Other Pagans in America by Margot Adler (Penguin Books, 2006)

The Elements of Ritual: Air, Fire, Water & Earth in the Wiccan Circle by Deborah Lipp (Llewellyn, 2003)

Magical Power for Beginners: How to Raise & Send Energy for Spells That Work by Deborah Lipp (Llewellyn, 2017)

Traditional Wicca: A Seeker's Guide by Thorn Mooney (Llewellyn, 2018)

CHAPTER 3: ASTROLOGY

Astro Gold (Cosmic Apps Pty): available on your phone or device's app store

Astrodienst: Astro.com, The World's Best Horoscopes (for chart drawing, analysis, and articles)

Astrology for Yourself: How to Understand and Interpret Your Own Birth Chart by Douglas Block and Demetra George (Ibis Press, 2006)

Astrology: Using the Wisdom of the Stars in Your Everyday Life by Carole Taylor (DK Publishing, 2018)

China Highlights, "Chinese Zodiac Signs": ChinaHighlights.com /travelguide/chinese-zodiac

Hellenistic Astrology: The Study of Fate and Fortune by Chris Brennan (Amor Fati Publications, 2017)

Llewellyn's Daily Planetary Guide (published annually by Llewellyn)

"Master Tsai Chinese Five Element Astrology": ChineseFortuneCalendar .com/Chineseastrology.htm

TimePassages (AstroGraph Software): available on your phone or device's app store

CHAPTER 4: NUMEROLOGY

Cheiro's Book of Numbers by Cheiro (Ancient Wisdom Publications, 2015) (Chaldean)

The Complete Book of Numerology: Discovering the Inner Self by David A. Phillips (Hay House, 2005) (Pythagorean)

Sacred Geometry: An A-Z Reference Guide by Marilyn Walker (Rockridge Press, 2020)

CHAPTER 5: ALCHEMY

Ancient Astrology, "The Planetary Rulership of Plants": AncientAstrology
.org/articles-/the-planetary-rulership-of-plants

Alchemy Lab, planetary charts: AlchemyLab.com/planetary_charts.htm

Alchemy & Mysticism: The Hermetic Museum by Alexander Roob
(Taschen, 2014)

The Alchemy Reader: From Hermes Trismegistus to Isaac Newton, edited by
Stanton J. Linden (Cambridge University Press, 2003)

The Complete Idiot's Guide to Alchemy by Dennis William Hauck (Alpha
Books, 2008)

Cunningham's Encyclopedia of Magical Herbs by Scott Cunningham
(Llewellyn, 8th ed., 2003)

Esoterica, the YouTube channel of Dr. Justin Sledge: YouTube.com
/channel/UCoydhtfFSk1fZXNRnkGnneQ

The Secrets of Alchemy by Lawrence M. Principe (The University of
Chicago Press, 2012)

Sorcerer's Stone: A Beginner's Guide to Alchemy by Dennis William Hauck
(Crucible Books, 2013)

CHAPTER 6: KABBALAH

777 and Other Qabalistic Writings of Aleister Crowley by Aleister Crowley
(Weiser Books, 1982)

A Garden of Pomegranates: Skrying on the Tree of Life by Israel Regardie
(Llewellyn, 1995)

The Mystic Quest: An Introduction to Jewish Mysticism by David S. Ariel
(Rowman & Littlefield, 1988)

The Mystical Qabalah by Dion Fortune (Weiser Books, 2000)

Qabalah for Wiccans: Ceremonial Magic on the Pagan Path by Jack Chanek
(Llewellyn, 2021)

The Shining Paths: An Experiential Journey Through the Tree of Life by Dolores Ashcroft-Nowicki (Thoth Publications, 1997)

CHAPTER 7: CEREMONIAL MAGIC

20th Century Magic and the Old Religion: Dion Fortune, Christine Hartley, Charles Seymour by Alan Richardson (Llewellyn, 1991)

The Astrum Argentium: AstrumArgenteum.org/en/home/

The Book of the Law by Aleister Crowley (Weiser Books, 1987)

Builder of the Adytum: BOTA.org

The Essential Enochian Grimoire: An Introduction to Angel Magick from Dr. John Dee to the Golden Dawn by Aaron Leitch (Llewellyn, 2014)

Foundations of High Magick: The Magical Philosophy by Melita Denning and Osborne Phillips (Book Sales, 2000)

Grimoires: A History of Magic Books by Owen Davies (Oxford University Press, 2009)

The Hermetic Order of the Golden Dawn: HermeticGoldenDawn.org

Liber Null & Psychonaut: An Introduction to Chaos Magic by Peter J. Carroll (Weiser Books, 1987)

Modern Magick: Eleven Lessons in the High Magickal Arts (Second Edition) by Donald Michael Kraig (Llewellyn, 1988)

Ordo Templi Orientis: OTO.org

Sigil Maker (Ikapel Media): available on your phone or device's app store

The Society of Inner Light: InnerLight.org.uk

Sword of Wisdom: MacGregor Mathers and the Golden Dawn by Ithell Colquhoun (G.P. Putnam's Sons, 1975)

Women of the Golden Dawn: Rebels and Priestesses by Mary K. Greer (Park Street Press, 1995)

CHAPTER 8: TAROT

Aeclectic Tarot (the most illustrated and possibly the largest collection of tarot reviews in the world): Aeclectic.net

Labyrinthos (decks and articles): Labyrinthos.co

Mastering the Tarot: Basic Lessons in an Ancient, Mystic Art by Eden Gray (Crown, 1973)

Pamela Colman Smith: The Untold Story by Stuart R. Kaplan with Mary K. Greer, Elizabeth Foley O'Connor, and Melinda Boyd Parsons (U.S. Games Systems, 2018)

Queer Tarot: List of Queer Tarot Decks: QueerTarot.cards/list-of-queer -tarot-decks

Seventy-Eight Degrees of Wisdom: A Tarot Journey to Self-Awareness by Rachel Pollack (Weiser, 2019)

Tarot Garden (sorted by topic): TarotGarden.com

Tarot Interactions: Become More Intuitive, Psychic & Skilled at Reading Cards by Deborah Lipp (Llewellyn Publications, 2015)

Tarot Magic: Ceremonial Magic Using Golden Dawn Correspondences by Donald Tyson (Llewellyn, 2018)

Tarot Spells by Janina Renée (Llewellyn, 2000)

Tarot Spreads: Layouts & Techniques to Empower Your Readings by Barbara Moore (Llewellyn, 2012)

Understanding the Tarot Court by Mary K. Greer and Tom Little (Llewellyn, 2004)

REFERENCES

Adler, Margot. *Drawing Down the Moon: Witches, Druids, Goddess-Worshippers and Other Pagans in America*. New York: Penguin Books, 2006.

Agrippa, Heinrich Cornelius, and Donald Tyson (ed). *Three Books of Occult Philosophy: The Foundation Book of Western Occultism*. Portland, OR: Llewellyn, 2018.

Ask Astrologer. "Pythagoras Numerology." Accessed February 20, 2021. AskAstrologer.com/pythagoras-numero.html#.

Astro Databank. "Adams, Evangeline." Accessed March 10, 2021. Astro .com/astro-databank/Adams,_Evangeline.

Attrell, Dan, and David Porreca (trans). *Picatrix: A Medieval Treatise on Astral Magic*. Written by Maslama ibn Ahmad al-Majriti. University Park, PA: Penn State University Press, 2019.

Barrett, Frances. *The Magus: A Complete System of Occult Philosophy*. York Beach, ME: Weiser, 2000.

Bayit: Building Jewish. "The Four Worlds." Accessed April 4, 2021. Your Bayit.org/the-four-worlds.

BecVar, Brent. "Introduction to Jyotish: Vedic Astrology." Chopra. November 7, 2013. Chopra.com/articles/introduction-to-jyotish -vedic-astrology.

Betz, Hans Dieter (ed). *The Greek Magical Papyri in Translation, Including the Demotic Spells*. Chicago: University of Chicago Press, 1986.

Beyer, Catherine. "Alchemical Sulfur, Mercury, and Salt in Western Occultism." Learn Religions. Updated July 3, 2019. LearnReligions.com /alchemical-sulfur-mercury-and-salt-96036.

Beyer, Catherine. "Planetary Intelligence Sigils of Western Occult Tradition." Learn Religions. Updated December 7, 2017. LearnReligions.com /planetary-intelligence-sigils-4123076.

Beyer, Catherine. "Planetary Magical Squares." Learn Religions. Updated January 20, 2019. LearnReligions.com/planetary-magical -squares-4123077.

Blackledge, Catherine, "The Man Who Saw The Future—A Biography of William Lilly: The 17th-Century Astrologer Who Changed the Course of the English Civil War." Astrodienst. Accessed February 11, 2021. Astro.com/astrology/in_lilly_e.htm.

Blyth, Maria. "Pamela Colman Smith: Tarot's High Priestess." *Cunning Folk*. October 29, 2020. Cunning-Folk.com/read-posts/pamela-colman -smith-tarots-high-priestess.

Bonewits, Isaac. *Witchcraft: A Concise Guide*. Earth Religions Press, 2003.

Bonner, Anthony. *The Art and Logic of Ramon Llull: A User's Guide*. Leiden, Netherlands: Brill, 2007.

Budge, E. A. Wallis. *Egyptian Magic*. Charleston, SC: BiblioBazaar, 2008.

Bustamonte, Star. "Two Projects Bring Attention to 'Witch-Hunts.'" *The Wild Hunt*. February 10, 2021. WildHunt.org/2021/02/two-projects -bring-attention-to-witch-hunts.html.

Cafe Astrology. "Numerology." Accessed March 2, 2021. CafeAstrology .com/numerology.html.

Carl Jung Resources. "Jung and Alchemy." Accessed March 20, 2021. Carl-Jung.net/alchemy.html.

Cheiro. *Cheiro's Book of Numbers*. Toronto, Canada: Ancient Wisdom Publications, 2015.

Chinese Fortune Calendar. "Master Tsai Chinese Five Element Astrology." Accessed March 30, 2021. ChineseFortuneCalendar.com /Chineseastrology.htm.

Christino, Karen. "A Brief Biography of Evangeline Adams." *Skyscript*. Accessed March 30, 2021. Skyscript.co.uk/adams.html.

Conniff, Richard. "Alchemy May Not Have Been the Pseudoscience We All Thought It Was." *Smithsonian Magazine*. February 2014. SmithsonianMag.com/history/alchemy-may-not-been-pseudoscience -we-thought-it-was-180949430.

Credo Quia Absurdum. "The Seven Stages of Alchemy." February 19, 2019. QuiaAbsurdum.com/the-seven-stages-of-alchemy.

Cunningham, Scott. *Cunningham's Encyclopedia of Magical Herbs*. Portland, OR: Llewellyn, 1987.

Cunningham, Scott. *Wicca: A Guide for the Solitary Practitioner*. Portland, OR: Llewellyn, 1989.

Denisoff, Dennis. "The Hermetic Order of the Golden Dawn, 1888-1901." *BRANCH*. January 2013. BranchCollective.org/?ps_articles=dennis -denisoff-the-hermetic-order-of-the-golden-dawn-1888-1901.

Encyclopaedia Britannica Online. s.v. "Helena Blavatasky: Russian Spiritualist." Accessed April 5, 2021. Britannica.com/biography /Helena-Blavatsky.

Edwards, Steven A. "Paracelsus, the Man Who Brought Chemistry to Medicine." *The American Association for the Advancement of Science*. March 2, 2012. AAAS.org/paracelsus-man-who-brought-chemistry -medicine.

Encyclopedia.com. "Zosimos Of Panopolis." Accessed March 19, 2021. Encyclopedia.com/science/dictionaries-thesauruses-pictures-and -press-releases/zosimos-panopolis.

English, Ali. "First Steps in Alchemy—Spagyric Tincture Making with Meadowsweet." The Eldrum Tree (blog). August 25, 2015. Eldrum .co.uk/2015/08/25/first-steps-in-alchemy-spagyric-tincture-making -with-meadowsweet.

Enter Alchemy (blog). "Spagyric Elixirs Pt. 1: Planetary Hours and Maceration." Accessed March 20, 2021. EnterAlchemy.wordpress .com/2014/03/12/spagyric-elixirs-pt-1-planetary-hours-and -maceration.

Enter Alchemy (blog). "Spagyric Elixirs Pt. 2: Calcination." Accessed March 20, 2021. EnterAlchemy.wordpress.com/2014/03/12/spagyric -elixirs-pt-2-calcination.

Enter Alchemy (blog). "Spagyric Elixirs Pt. 3: Further Calcination and Cohobation." Accessed March 20, 2021. EnterAlchemy.wordpress .com/2014/03/14/spagyric-elixirs-pt-3-further-calcination-and -cohobation.

Evolved Alchemy. "What is Spagyrics?" Accessed March 22, 2021. EvolvedAlchemy.com/what-is-spagyrics.

Faulkner, Kevin. "Scintillae Marginila: Sparkling Margins—Alchemical and Hermetic Thought in the Literary Works of Sir Thomas Browne." The Alchemy Web Site. 2002. Levity.com/alchemy/sir_thomas _browne.html.

Fletcher, Karhlyle. "Spagyric Cannabis Extraction Offers True, Full-Spectrum Tinctures." Cannabis Tech. March 5, 2020. CannabisTech .com/articles/spagyric-cannabis-extraction-offers-true-full-spectrum -tinctures.

Fortune, Dion. *The Mystical Qabalah*. York Beach, ME: Weiser Books, 2000.

Frazer, Sir James George. *The New Golden Bough: A New Abridgment of the Classic Work*. New York: Criterion Books, 1959.

Freeman, Tzvi. "Da'at: The Knowing I." Chabad.org. Accessed April 4, 2021. Chabad.org/library/article_cdo/aid/299648/jewish/Daat.htm.

Fulgur. "Austin Osman Spare." Accessed April 10, 2021. fulgur.co.uk /artists-and-writers/austin-osman-spare.

Gardner, Gerald Brousseau. *Witchcraft Today*. New York: Citadel Press, 2004.

Ghost City Tours blog. "Marie Laveau, the Voodoo Queen of New Orleans." Accessed March 1, 2021. GhostCityTours.com/new-orleans/marie -laveau/.

Guiley, Rosemary Ellen. *The Encyclopedia of Magic and Alchemy*. New Milford, CT: Visionary Living, 2006.

Guiley, Rosemary Ellen. *The Encyclopedia of Witches and Witchcraft*. New York: Facts on File, 1989.

Guinness World Records. "Most Accurate Value of Pi." Accessed April 23, 2021. GuinnessWorldRecords.com/world-records/66179-most -accurate-value-of-pi.

Hames, Harvey J. *The Art of Conversion: Christianity and Kabbalah in the Thirteenth Century*. Leiden, Netherlands: Brill, 2000.

Hauck, Dennis William. *Sorcerer's Stone: A Beginner's Guide to Alchemy*. New York: Citadel Press, 2004.

Heselton, Philip. *Witchfather: A Life of Gerald Gardner* (Vols. 1 and 2). Leicestershire, UK: Thoth Publications, 2012.

Hoeller, Stephan A. "C. G. Jung and the Alchemical Renewal." The Gnosis Archive. Accessed March 20, 2021. Gnosis.org/jung_alchemy.htm.

Honorius of Thebes and Joseph Peterson (trans). *The Sworn Book of Honorius: Liber Iuratus Honorii*. Lake Worth, FL: Ibis Press, 2016.

Horn, Mark. "Kabbalah, Cabala or Qabalah: What's Up with These Different Spellings?" Gates of Light Tarot (blog). January 11, 2018. GatesOfFlightTarot.com/blog/2017/9/3/kabbalah-cabala-or-qabbalah -whats-up-with-all-these-different-spellings.

Hutton, Ronald. *The Triumph of the Moon: A History of Modern Pagan Witchcraft*. Oxford: Oxford University Press, 1999.

Javed, Syed Tariq. "Cheiro, a Mysterious Palmist." Horus, the Astro-Palmist (blog). July 20, 2016. HorusAstroPalmist.wordpress.com/tag/count -louis-hamon.

Jewish Virtual Library. "Gematria." Accessed February 20, 2021. Jewish VirtualLibrary.org/gematria-2.

Jewish Virtual Library. "Isaac Ben Solomon Luria (1534–1572)." Accessed April 3, 2021. JewishVirtualLibrary.org/isaac-ben-solomon-luria.

Jewish Virtual Library. "Kabbalah: The Zohar." Accessed April 3, 2021. JewishVirtualLibrary.org/the-zohar.

Jiang, Fercility. "Chinese Zodiac." China Highlights. March 22, 2021. ChinaHighlights.com/travelguide/chinese-zodiac.

Kaczynski, Richard. *Perdurabo: The Life of Aleister Crowley*. Berkeley, CA: North Atlantic Books, 2010.

Kaplan, Stuart R. *The Encyclopedia of the Tarot: Volume 1*. Stamford, CT: U.S. Games Systems, 1978.

Konraad, Sandor. *Numerology: Key to the Tarot*. Whitford Press, 1983.

Kraig, Donald Michael. *Modern Magick: Eleven Lessons in the High Magickal Arts*. 2nd ed. Portland, OR: Llewellyn, 1988.

Labyrinthos. "The Seven Stages of Alchemical Transformation: A Spiritual Metaphor (Infographic)." Labyrinthos blog. December 9, 2016. Labyrinthos.co/blogs/learn-tarot-with-labyrinthos-academy /the-seven-stages-of-alchemical-transformation-a-spiritual -metaphor-infographic.

Leiberman, Shimon. "Kabbala #9: Daat – The Bridge Between Idea and Reality." Aish.com. Accessed April 4, 2021. Aish.com/sp/k /Kabbala_9_Daat_-_The_Bridge_Between_Idea_and_Reality.html.

Leitch, Aaron. *The Essential Enochian Grimoire: An Introduction to Angel Magick from Dr. John Dee to the Golden Dawn*. Portland, OR: Llewellyn, 2014.

Leland, Charles Geoffrey. *Aradia: Gospel of the Witches*. Blaine, WA: Phoenix Publishing, 1990.

LGBT Health & Wellbeing. "An Interview with Trans Icon Rachel Pollack." Accessed April 7, 2021. LGBTHealth.org.uk/lgbt-health-blog/interview -rachel-pollack.

Lindahl, Carl, John McNamara, and John Lindow, ed. *Medieval Folklore: A Guide to Myths, Legends, Tales, Beliefs, and Customs*. New York: Oxford University Press, 2002.

Masé, Guido. "A Brief Recipe for Making a Spagyric Extract of Peppermint (Mentha piperita)." Vermont Center for Integrative Herbalism. Accessed March 20, 2021. VTHerbCenter.org/wp-content/uploads/2012 /04/A-brief-recipe-for-making-a-spagyric-extract-of-Peppermint.pdf.

Mathers, Samuel Liddell MacGregor (trans). *The Goetia: The Lesser Key of Solomon the King (Clavicula Salomonis Regis)*. York Beach, ME: Weiser, 1995.

Mathers, Samuel Liddell MacGregor (trans). *The Key of Solomon the King (Clavicula Salomonis)*. York Beach, ME: Weiser, 2000.

Means, Ja'Quintin. "Famous Alchemist: Zosimos of Panopolis." The Wondering Alchemist (blog). April 2, 2020. TheWonderingAlchemist.com /blog/famous-alchemist-zosimos-of-panopolis.

Medieval Life and Times. "Medieval Craft Guilds." Accessed April 5, 2021. Medieval-Life-And-Times.info/medieval-england/medieval-craft -guilds.htm.

Mehrtens, Sue. "Jung on Numbers." Jungian Center for the Spiritual Sciences. Accessed February 12, 2021. JungianCenter.org/jung-on -numbers.

Melton, J. Gordon. "Rosicrucian: Religion." In *Encyclopaedia Britannica Online*. Accessed April 5, 2021. Britannica.com/topic/Rosicrucians.

Mer-Amun. "What is 'Pathworking'?" Dreaming at the Feet of Hades. August 2008. DreamingHades.com/articles/pathworking/what-is -pathworking.

Metzger, Jane. "How To Make Herbal Glycerites: Tinctures Without Alcohol." *The Herbal Academy*. April 30, 2014. TheHerbalAcademy .com/how-to-make-herbal-glycerites-tinctures-without-alcohol.

Modern Ghana. "Akua Denteh Foundation Inaugurated." September 1, 2020. ModernGhana.com/news/1026751/akua-denteh-foundation -inaugurated.html.

Montufar, Narayana. "The Revival of Traditional Astrology: An Interview with Chris Brennan." Astrology.com. January 17, 2020. Astrology.com /article/traditional-astrology-revival-chris-brennan-interview.

Murray, Margaret Alice. *The Witch-Cult in Western Europe: A Study in Anthropology*. London, UK: Aziloth Books, 2019.

The National Archives. "A Witch's Confession." Accessed February 16, 2021. NationalArchives.gov.uk/education/resources/early-modern -witch-trials/a-witchs-confession.

Patterson, Steve. *Cecil Williamson's Book of Witchcraft: A Grimoire of the Museum of Witchcraft*. Woodbury, MN: Llewellyn, 2020.

Pelham, Libby. "The Biography of Evangeline Adams." Explore Astrology. Updated June 16, 2016. ExploreAstrology.co.uk /thebiographyofevangelineadams.html.

Pitzl-Waters, Jason. "Donald Michael Kraig 1951 – 2014." The Wild Hunt. March 18, 2014. WildHunt.org/2014/03/donald-michael-kraig-1951 -2014.html.

Pollack, Rachel. "Rachel Pollack." Accessed April 7, 2021. RachelPollack .com/bio.

Pollack, Rachel. *Seventy-Eight Degrees of Wisdom: A Tarot Journey to Self-Awareness*. 3rd ed., revised. Newburyport, MA: Weiser Books, 2019.

Professional Numerology (blog). "Pythagorean Numerology." Accessed February 20, 2021. ProfessionalNumerology.com /pythagoreansystem.html.

Ratzabi, Hila. "What Is Gematria?" My Jewish Learning. Accessed February 20, 2021. MyJewishLearning.com/article/gematria.

Ray, Sharmistha. "Reviving a Forgotten Artist of the Occult." Hyperallergic. March 23, 2019. Hyperallergic.com/490918/pamela-colman-smith -pratt-institute-libraries.

Regardie, Israel. *The Golden Dawn: The Original Account of the Teachings, Rites & Ceremonies of the Hermetic Order*. Portland, OR: Llewellyn, 2002.

Richardson, Alan. *20th Century Magic and the Old Religion: Dion Fortune, Christine Hartley, Charles Seymour*. St. Paul, MN: Llewellyn, 1991.

Robinson, George. "Isaac Luria and Kabbalah in Safed." My Jewish Learning. Accessed April 3, 2021. MyJewishLearning.com/article/isaac -luria-kabbalah-in-safed.

Roya, Will. "The History of Playing Cards: The Evolution of the Modern Deck." PlayingCardDecks.com. October 16, 2018. PlayingCardDecks .com/blogs/all-in/history-playing-cards-modern-deck.

Scarborough, Samuel. "The Vibratory Formula and Its Use in Daily Ritual Work." *Journal of the Western Mystery Tradition* 5, no. 1 (Autumnal Equinox 2003). JWMT.org/v1n5/vibratoryform.html.

Shuttleworth, Martyn. "Ancient Chinese Alchemy." Explorable. May 25, 2010. Explorable.com/chinese-alchemy.

Sledge, Justin. "Alchemy - Maria the Jewess & Prophet - Greco Egyptian Alchemy & Hermetic Philosophy." Esoterica. YouTube video, 27:38. March 12, 2021. YouTu.be/pRb9vwk14OA.

The Society of Inner Light. "Home." Accessed April 5, 2021. InnerLight .org.uk.

Sol, Mateo. "7 Stages of Spiritual Alchemy." Lonerwolf. Updated June 12, 2021. LonerWolf.com/spiritual-alchemy.

Sotheby's. "8 Things to Know About Chinese Numerology." Sotheby's blog. September 10, 2018. Sothebys.com/chinese-numerology-explained -with-diamonds.

Spooky Scotland. "Isobel Gowdie: A Witch Trial Extraordinaire in Auldearn, Scotland." Accessed February 15, 2021. SpookyScotland.net /isobel-gowdie.

Stanford Encyclopedia of Philosophy. "Heinrich Cornelius Agrippa von Nettesheim." Updated March 18, 2021. Plato.stanford.edu/entries /agrippa-nettesheim.

Stanford Encyclopedia of Philosophy. "Pythagoras." Updated October 17, 2018. Plato.stanford.edu/entries/pythagoras.

Stavish, Mark. "Practical Plant Alchemy—Part One." Alchemy Web Site. 1996. Accessed March 10, 2021. AlchemyWebsite.com/plant1.html.

Suster, Gerald. *Crowley's Apprentice: The Life and Ideas of Israel Regardie.* York Beach, ME: Weiser Books, 1990.

Telushkin, Joseph. "Kabbalah: An Overview." Jewish Virtual Library. Accessed April 3, 2021. JewishVirtualLibrary.org/kabbalah-an -overview.

Temple of the Good Game. "Kameoth of the Planets Ancient and Modern." Accessed March 2, 2021. GoodGame.org.nz/kameas.html.

Travel China Guide. "Chinese Zodiac Years Chart." Accessed March 30, 2021. TravelChinaGuide.com/intro/chinese-zodiac-years-chart.htm.

Trismegistus, Hermes. *The Corpus Hermeticum: Initiation Into Hermetics, The Hermetica Of Hermes Trismegistus.* Pantianos Classics, 2016.

Trismegistus, Hermes. *The Emerald Tablet of Hermes.* Merchant Books, 2013.

Waite, Arthur Edward. *The Pictorial Key to the Tarot: Being Fragments of a Secret Tradition under the Veil of Divination.* York Beach, ME: Weiser Books, 1990.

Warwick, Tarl (ed). *Grimoirium Verum: The True Grimoire*. CreateSpace Independent Publishing Platform, 2015.

Wigington, Patti. "Ceremonial Magic." Learn Religions. Updated November 29, 2017. LearnReligions.com/ceremonial-magic-p2 -2561878.

The Wizarding World Team. "The Real Nicolas Flamel and the Philosopher's Stone." Wizarding World. July 6, 2020. WizardingWorld.com /features/the-real-nicolas-flamel-and-the-philosophers-stone.

Wright, Jaime. "Chinese Zodiac Elements: How to Know What Yours Is and What It Means." Pure Wow. February 9, 2021. PureWow.com /wellness/chinese-zodiac-elements.

Yeromiyan, Tania. "An Introduction to Chinese Numerology." Chinese Language Institute (CLI). Updated April 26, 2021. StudyCLI.org /chinese-culture/chinese-numerology/.

INDEX

H

Harris, Frieda, 148
Healing, 12–14
Hebrew numerology, 74–75
Hellenistic astrology, 56
Hermetica, xiv–xv, 99
Hermeticism, xiv–xv
Hermetic Order of the
 Golden Dawn, 102, 121, 127, 136
Heselton, Philip, 27
Hoodoo, 10–11
Hopkins, Matthew, 25
Horary astrology, 58
Horoscopes
 about, 41
 aspects, 52–53
 elements, 46–47
 houses, 45–46
 planets, 43–44
 qualities, 46–47
 zodiac signs, 42
Hutton, Ronald, 9, 20

I

Imitative magic, 5
Inner work, 131–132
Invocation, 134–135

J

Jabir ibn Hayyan. *See* Geber
Judaism. *See* Kabbalah
Jung, Carl, 63, 64, 84, 146
Jyotish astrology, 57

K

Kabbalah
 about, 101–103, 117
 Christian, 112
 Hermetic, 112–113

hermetic, 117
Jewish, 111
magical uses, 113–115
numerology, 75
and tarot, 144–145
texts, 116
Tree of Life, 103–110
Karmic astrology, 54
Kelley, Edward, 126–127
Kraig, Donald Michael, 119, 125

L

Laveau, Marie, 11
Leland, Charles Godfrey, 25
Lenormand cards, 149–150
León, Moses de, 101
Lévi, Éliphas, 120, 140, 144, 148
Life path number, 76–77
Lilly, William, 58
*Llewellyn's Daily Planetary
 Guide,* 48
Llull, Ramon, 101
Lost objects, finding of, 15–16
Lunar rites, 32
Luria, Isaac, 111–112

M

Magic, 21. *See also* Ceremonial
 magic; Folk magic
Magical contagion, 4
Magic number squares, 78–79
Magnum Opus, 94–95
Magus, The (Barrett), 120
Mathematics, 65–68
Mather, Increase, 19
Mathers, Moina, 127, 129
Mathers, S. L. MacGregor, 127, 129
Matutina, Stella, 129
Medieval astrology, 56
Medieval Folklore, 12

Placing the Tree on
    Your Body, 110
  sephirot, 104–106
  triads, 106
Trismegistus, Hermes, 60, 91, 125
Trithemius, Johannes, 91
Triumph of the Moon, The
    (Hutton), 20

U

Uranian astrology, 54

V

Vibratory Formula, 133
Visconti-Sforza tarocchi
    deck, 140
Vodoun, xii, 11

W

Waite, Arthur Edward, 127, 129,
    140, 144, 146–147, 148
Warner, William John, 71
Westcott, William, 127
Western alchemy, 90–91
Wheel of the Year, 34
Wicca, xii, 23, 27–29, 137
Wicca (Cunningham), 29

Wirth, Oswald, 148
Witchcraft
  about, 19–20, 36
  depictions of, 24–29
  practices, 21–23, 29–30,
    32, 34–35
  religion and, 23
  tools, 31
  Wicca and, 27–29
Witchcraft Today (Gardner), 27
Witch-Cult in Western Europe,
    The (Murray), 20, 22
Witte, Alfred, 54
Women's International
    Terrorist Conspiracy from
    Hell (W.I.T.C.H.), 26
Woodman, W. R., 127
Words of power, 6–7

Y

Yeats, William Butler, 127, 129

Z

Zener cards, xiii–xiv
Zohar, The, 101, 103, 111
Zosimos, 84, 87

ACKNOWLEDGMENTS

My first book was dedicated to Susan Carberry. Shortly before I began writing this book, I learned she had passed away. She was an extraordinary woman; entirely self-taught, she dropped out of school at age 16, had one of the largest personal libraries I've ever seen, and eventually started her own business. She was a gifted astrologer, tarot reader, and witch.

Rabbi Leana Moritt introduced me to the work of Dr. Justin Sledge. Claudiney Prieto read the alchemy chapter for me and gave me helpful comments. Jack Chanek did the same for Kabbalah, and my daughter, Ursula Rising, was generous with her help on astrology. Anything I got wrong is definitely not their fault.

My beloved Professor Spouse took care of me in every way while I wrote. She's a gift.

I've written most of this book with my little one-eyed tuxedo cat in my lap. Callie is a very good girl.

ABOUT THE AUTHOR

DEBORAH LIPP is the author of 10 books, including *The Complete Book of Spells, Magical Power for Beginners, Tarot Interactions*, and *The Ultimate James Bond Fan Book*. (One of these things is not like the others.) Deborah has been teaching Wicca, magic, and the occult for more than 30 years. She became a Witch and High Priestess in the 1980s, as an initiate of the Gardnerian tradition. She has lectured on Pagan and occult topics on three continents.

In "real life" Deborah is a senior business analyst. She lives with Professor Spouse and an assortment of cats in Jersey City, New Jersey. Find her on Twitter and Instagram at @DebLippAuthor.

Printed in the USA
CPSIA information can be obtained
at www.ICGtesting.com
LVHW060433120124
768705LV00007B/36